# ENTERPRISE APPLICATIONS UNLOCKED

## LOW CODE NO CODE

## SRIRAM GANESHAN

INDIA • SINGAPORE • MALAYSIA

Copyright © Sriram Ganeshan 2024
All Rights Reserved.

ISBN
Paperback  979-8-89556-347-2
Hardcase  979-8-89556-816-3

This book has been published with all efforts taken to make the material error-free after the consent of the author. However, the author and the publisher do not assume and hereby disclaim any liability to any party for any loss, damage, or disruption caused by errors or omissions, whether such errors or omissions result from negligence, accident, or any other cause.

While every effort has been made to avoid any mistake or omission, this publication is being sold on the condition and understanding that neither the author nor the publishers or printers would be liable in any manner to any person by reason of any mistake or omission in this publication or for any action taken or omitted to be taken or advice rendered or accepted on the basis of this work. For any defect in printing or binding the publishers will be liable only to replace the defective copy by another copy of this work then available.

# Contents

# Foreword

**Suresh Sambandam**
Founder & CEO, Kissflow

The business world is undergoing a remarkable shift, driven by rapid digital transformation and the need for agility. For organizations to thrive in this fast-paced environment, they need to move beyond traditional methods of software development. Enter Low-Code and No-Code platforms—revolutionary tools that democratize the development process, enabling even non-technical users to build and deploy solutions with minimal input from IT. This book is your guide to navigating this new landscape.

Whether you're an IT leader aiming to enhance operational efficiency or a business executive seeking to empower your teams, this book has been written for you. As the demand for digital solutions grows, so does the need for agile, scalable, and innovative tools. In many organizations, it is the IT leaders spearheading the implementation of these platforms, while in others, digital transformation teams are driving the change. Regardless of your role or region, this book is here to provide the clarity and insights you need to successfully adopt Low-Code, No-Code, or Citizen Development platforms.

Throughout the following chapters, you'll explore the critical steps required to implement these platforms effectively. From understanding why these tools are crucial in today's business environment, to selecting the right platform, aligning organizational goals, and measuring ROI, this book will serve as a strategic roadmap. You'll also learn how to identify the right types of projects, especially those well-suited for citizen development, and understand how to expand success into a long-term practice within your organization.

Whether you're just beginning your journey with Low-Code and No-Code or looking to scale up, the guidance provided in these pages will equip you with the knowledge and strategies to make the most of these powerful platforms. Let this book inspire you to lead your organization into the next phase of digital transformation.

Embrace the future—where innovation knows no bounds.

# Chapter 1

# Need for Low Code and No Code

*What if you could compose your own songs without learning music or how to play any musical instruments?*

Music is a great form of art. We all like music, one genre or another. Some of us can play instruments, and others can sing. Very few can compose music, but all of us like music.

Imagine if you had the power to compose and create music you like yourself without learning any form of music or any instruments. Would that not be awesome?

It would certainly be transformational, but we don't have this yet. What if I were to tell you something similar is available to help you with your work?

Yes, you can simplify and automate work for you and for your team or company by building your own applications. This is without learning programming languages or without learning any software development tools.

All you need is an understanding of processes and the business outcomes you are looking to achieve.

This is being made possible today using low code and citizen development platforms. Before diving into the world of low code, no code, let's take a step back to understand the origins of this concept.

A pioneer in personal software and services is Bill Gates, who said, "The advance of technology is based on making it fit in so that you don't even notice it, so it's part of everyday life."

The statement above signifies the exponential evolution of technology and the seamless absorption of the same into our lives. From Apple to Google to Facebook to Amazon to Uber to Netflix to Generative AI, technology has not stopped surprising us. If you look at one common thread among all these technological advancements, it is the ability of technology to simplify our day-to-day lives.

A sophisticated web of components in the backend that delivers simple yet powerful experiences at the front end.

All this is on the consumer side. When we look at the technology landscape for businesses, the scene is slightly different. Of course, business technology landscapes have also evolved significantly, and I do not intend to take away any credit from that. It is also true that consumer tech and business/enterprise tech are interconnected and influence each other.

However, it is widely acknowledged that the evolution of business technology has been slower compared to consumer technology. There are several factors contributing to this:

Consumer adoption rates are much higher and faster. People are quick to adopt newer applications and gadgets that are of value to them, and barriers to change for individuals are low.

Competition Landscape: The consumer market is extremely competitive, and since experiences are easily replicable and imitable, the adoption and consumer feedback lead to continuous innovation, focus on user experience, and rapid product development.

Influence of Trends: Consumer technology is driven by trends and fads and needs to cater quickly to evolving demands.

Business technology, on the other hand, cannot move so swiftly.

Adoption of new technology is slow and requires consensus and management support, often difficult to achieve.

Concerns of reliability, scalability, and security must be evaluated and addressed before any changes are introduced.

New changes need to assimilate into the existing ecosystem through integrations, and that may throw up several challenges in terms of compatibility and architecture.

Even if all these challenges are overcome, implementation cycles are long, laborious, and expensive.

Business user experiences and best practices are not commonly available for display as they would be in the case of consumer products, and therefore are harder to create and replicate.

Like I said before, despite these challenges, enterprise/business technology has taken significant strides forward, but still has a long way to go.

In many ways, we are today standing at an inflection point in the history of business technology. A significant portion of consumer-facing technology for all major and successful businesses today is on a modern technology stack, providing decent to excellent consumer experience through the front-end applications. The same organizations still struggle with slow and mediocre backend systems that are crumbling to cope with the pressure from the front end.

The pressure on the systems invariably also reflects on the people in those organizations, causing frustration and demotivation.

Most organizations today do realize this and have embarked on a quest to transform digitally. Yes, one of the most abused terms is Digital Transformation.

But in order for such initiatives to work, organizations need miracles. They need an army of developers who can understand business requirements and deliver fully integrated applications with consumer-like experiences in days, if not weeks, and at very low costs.

That sounds like not one but several miracles.

I am reminded of the project management triangle, illustrated below, that I am sure many of us would have come across before. Scope, Cost, and Time are levers that control quality, and when you cannot compromise on any of those levers, you forfeit your control of quality.

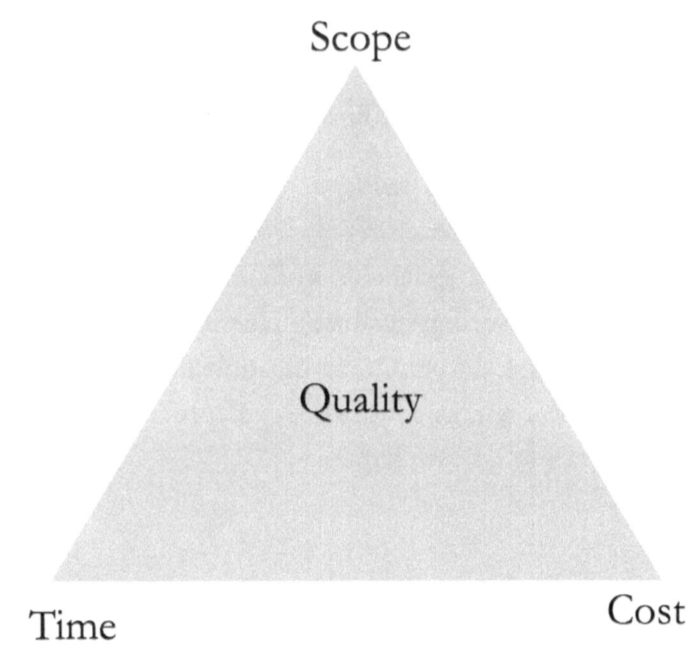



*Fig 1.1*

So what does one do?

I believe this stalemate has been the source of the evolution of many modern-day enterprise technology formulations. From

COTS (commercial off-the-shelf) applications to SaaS (Software as a Service) to Microservices-based Architecture, many others are all ways to optimize one or more of these three levers.

The evolution of COTS also meant that enterprises were challenged with a new dilemma: Build vs. Buy.

While the Build approach  meant greater control and adherence to requirements, the Buy Approach  leverages availability of prebuilt applications for specific purposes that provided faster time to market and lower costs on most occasions.

Whenever we have a problem with two completely divergent views, the solution is usually found somewhere in the middle, between the extremes of the problem or argument. Evolution of Low Code No Code was that solution.

It provided businesses with a way to look at the Build approach without compromising on costs, timeline, and quality. It also provided a way to enable collaborative fusion teams for development, empowering business stakeholders to play a more hands-on role in the development of applications. This has now evolved and is known as Citizen Development, which will be discussed in detail in a later chapter.

# Chapter 2

# Definition and Types of Low Code No Code Platforms

*Life is full of choices, just like a bakery is full of cakes.*
*Choose your flavor and savor every bite.*

While there are many definitions of Low Code No Code, the one that I most relate to is Forrester's definition: "No code Low Code development platforms empower business and IT teams to rapidly build applications with little to no hand-coding, using visual interfaces, drag-and-drop tools, and model-driven logic through declarative approaches."

It mandates a visual interface-driven application-building process but allows room for little coding, and most importantly, it calls out the role of both the business and the IT teams.

However, it may not be wise to paint all platforms available in this space with the same brush.

Low Code No Code is an approach to application building. It is also evolving and maturing as time passes by. Many different types of platforms have emerged during this time, and it is important to understand the variations to make the right choices.

Below are some major types of platforms I have come across. The list and specialty are growing as low code explores its boundaries.

## *Business Process Automation Platforms:*

Business process automation platforms have been around for a long time now. Early workflow systems could be traced back to the 1980s when systems focused on routing tasks between users and departments. Sounds familiar?

This was followed by an era of business re-engineering, where the concept of optimizing business processes to achieve improvements in performance and productivity gained prominence. Six Sigma, Lean, Continuous Improvement, and other approaches guided the evolution of BPM solutions during this time.

The next phase saw the rise of comprehensive BPM Suites with process modeling capabilities, process automation, and integration capabilities. The focus was on integrating and seamless communication with other applications in the ecosystem.

As Digital Transformation gained momentum, and Low Code No Code gained popularity, BPM seemed a natural fit for many vendors. No Code BPM is a powerful tool in the hands of both IT and business, more so for the business stakeholders. Powerful drag-and-drop-based techniques to quickly build forms and workflows meant that business stakeholders with no IT skills could easily automate and maintain their processes.

It is noteworthy here that Robotic Process Automation, Intelligent Document Processing, and Content Process Automation are areas where platforms provide capabilities that may be critical to business process automation.

Some low code platforms have already expanded their capabilities to include these functions, while others provide effective integration mechanisms to existing market leaders in this space.

The BPM space is also evolving, and the future is shifting from rule-based decisions to ML-based decision models. The advent of Generative AI has thrown a new challenge at all BPM platforms, including those with No Code capabilities. Platforms that make effective and useful adoption of AI/ML models into BPM would have a great advantage in this crowded red ocean of BPM providers.

## *Integration Low Code Platforms:*

Integration has been a challenge and in many ways a roadblock for change in business architecture landscapes. Compatibility, security, and scalability remain significant concerns even to this day. What has also been a major challenge is the need for highly skilled developers to perform integrations.

This need or pain point has been captured well by the modern-day low code integration platforms that seek to simplify the process of building and managing integrations, allowing users with lower skill sets to integrate using drag-and-drop approaches.

## *LCAP – Low Code Application Platform:*

Many of you might wonder what this type is. Aren't we talking about low code already and how could Low code be a type of Low Code No Code?

Your questions are valid, and this is where we need to get a little deeper into our understanding of Low Code No Code.

Low Code Application platforms are a variant within this space that require some degree of technical expertise to create applications. This is typically not for business users and is not suitable for Citizen Development.

Hang on a minute, is that not fundamentally against all that we have been proposing so far?

Well, yes and no – LCAP platforms have carved a niche and reputation for themselves in the space, and according to Gartner, they also have the biggest share of the pie among all types we will discuss here.

While they may not be fully drag-and-drop, they still provide effective means to reduce code and skills required to build complex applications. That may include sleek UI, custom mobile apps, complex integrations, and process orchestrations across systems. This also provides shorter development times, easier maintenance, lower costs, and significantly lower skill requirements when compared to traditional custom development approaches.

Obviously, these are not the right platforms to enable citizen development or even to automate processes of lower complexity. Not that they will not be able to automate, just that there would not be any advantage in terms of time savings.

The purpose of these platforms is to handle a higher degree of complexity and allow developers an easier and faster means to perform their work.

## CADP (Citizen Automation and Development):

Citizen Development or CADP platforms are the opposite of LCAP. They are completely No Code and very business-friendly. They allow for rapid application development by providing prebuilt templates and easy drag-and-drop approach-based tools to create workflows, forms, pages, and UI. They are very well-suited to enable users with different levels of skills to create and manage their applications.

Obviously, the level of abstraction that is needed to operationalize such platforms means there are inherent limitations. CADP platforms may not be able to handle all use cases that could be achieved through an LCAP platform.

Here I would also like to carefully draw the line between complex applications and business-critical applications and humbly point out that not all business-critical applications are complex technical use cases.

Business-critical applications could also be automated on CADP or No Code platforms. As these platforms also provide an equally robust infrastructure in terms of security, availability, and scalability. Therefore, the selection of a platform for any use case should be purely based on the capabilities required rather than the criticality of the application itself.

It is worth noting that several platforms in this domain have started incorporating extensibility features through open-source-based scripting mechanisms. This addition helps overcome certain limitations of pure drag-and-drop abstractions.

The involvement of business users in the development process is often met with caution and suspicion from IT stakeholders, and rightfully so, as it raises concerns about governance.

Citizen development operating models, governance approaches are developing at a rapid pace, and learnings from practical implementations are enriching these models. We will touch on some of these models in later chapters.

While Citizen Development Platforms could be a game-changer if implemented correctly, the adoption rates are still low as per many studies, despite their existence for a few years now.

In my view, it is not at all surprising, as they fundamentally change the way organizations work today.

The successful adoption of such platforms requires vision and support from leadership and an open-minded embrace from mid-management in organizations. That is easier said than done.


## *SaaS Extension Low Code Platforms:*

Software as a Service (SaaS), platforms or solutions, is now commonplace in most large organizations across the world. From

ERP to CRM to ITSM, there are many pioneers in this space that have completely overtaken the enterprise application landscape.

SaaS solutions inherently come with customization limitations and open up possibilities for other platforms to fill in the white spaces.

This is where low code platforms saw another opportunity to enter. Specific use cases where customization or extensibility was not possible or complex with SaaS, low code solutions would fit into it, providing the necessary functions and integrating to SaaS solutions to ensure continuity.

Major SaaS providers saw an opportunity here as well. While it was complicated for them to allow for such extensions in their core modules, they provided additional extension platforms to customize. They also provided ready-to-use connectors with their core platforms to ease integration efforts, hence improving their chances in the game.

While the jury is still out on whether the SaaS No Code Platforms would eventually eat up the space, or whether the niche low code providers would sustain their growth, the options for businesses are plenty, and that may not always be a good thing.

## *Multi-Experience Low Code Platforms (MLCAP):*

This is a type of low code platform that allows for the development of applications for multiple user experiences or devices. The aim is to enable a consistent user experience across channels and devices.

User Experience has been at the forefront of consumer products, and the advances in this space are for everyone to see. But behind the scenes, there is a lot of effort and handshakes between the business, the designers, and developers, and that always leads to miscommunications and misinterpretations.

So, building a good user experience across channels could be a costly and time-consuming affair. This is the pain that Multi-Experience LCAP tries to resolve.

With these platforms, business users and designers could also develop experiences using drag-and-drop approaches.

While this space is still evolving, the potential is enormous, and the niche would provide a first-mover advantage, at least for a brief period.

Along the same lines, we also have other types such as Rapid Mobile App development platforms and Rapid Web Development platforms, but my sense is that these will have to perish or expand to Multi-Experience to remain relevant and competitive in the market.

## *Domain-Specific Low Code Platforms:*

As the Low Code space expands with more and more new players entering the arena every day, USPs and differentiators become critical.

This is where several new players pick a niche based on their experience and introduce key industry or application capabilities into their platforms to give customers a head start while building on their platforms. This further reduces costs and enables organizations to focus on changes and maintenance rather than building from scratch.

This would be the second iteration of the Build vs. Buy debate where easily customizable COTS.

Organizations also feel comfortable working with vendors and platforms that understand the complexities, regulations, and nuances of their industry.

There are platforms already that are focused on industries such as BFSI, Healthcare, Education, and Manufacturing, all needing industry expertise in delivering applications.

I also see rising instances of platforms for specific application areas such as Procurement, Logistics, and HR. Yes, ideally, these would be considered core ERP functions, but if you get to customize them at lower costs, why not?

As we see, there are many varieties of low code no code platforms. Although this is a growing market, the competition is fierce. Many platforms are trying to occupy multiple positions to gain maximum market share, while some are focused on carving out a niche for themselves.

The consolidation in this space is still a few years away, in my view. But in the meantime, my humble suggestion to businesses is to keep an open mind.

Studies suggest that enterprises might adopt up to three low code and no code platforms concurrently to serve diverse purposes. As we progress, this number is expected to increase further. Moreover, the distinction between low code platforms and non-low code platforms/solutions is gradually becoming less defined, and over time, this convergence is likely to increase even more.

Under such circumstances, it is natural for organizations to be confused when choosing Low Code No Code platforms. How do I choose the right platform for my needs? This is exactly what we will address in the next chapter.

For Low Code No Code vendors, the opportunities for growth are plenty, but there is no room for mediocrity. Finding and focusing on developing USPs is key.

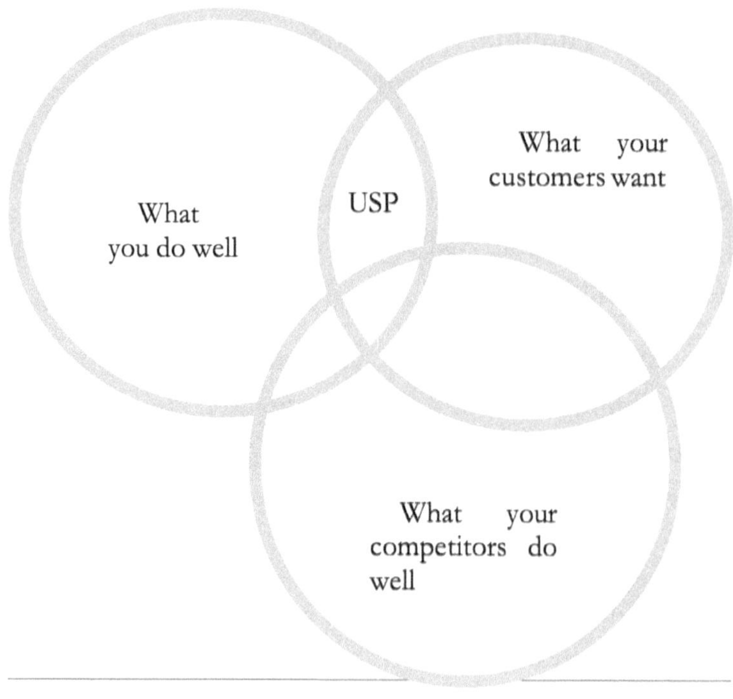


*Fig 2.1*

# Choosing the Right Platform

*Each organization is a snowflake, unique in its own way.*
*Choose wisely based on your own needs and priorities.*

Choosing a Low Code, No Code platform for an organization's needs would depend on the nature of requirements, strategic vision, and operational character of the organization, and therefore, there is no one-size-fits-all recipe to evaluate platforms.

However, there are several factors to consider that may act as guiding principles while choosing a Low Code No Code Platform.

## *No Code Vs Low Code Dilemma:*

The first major distinction and critical guiding factor is to consider what kind of users would play the creator or developer roles on the platform.

This is one of the most important considerations that may fundamentally qualify or disqualify platforms available in the Low Code/No Code landscape.

If you intend to have business users play a more active role in the design, creation, testing, and maintenance of artifacts on the platform, then you must choose a No Code or Citizen Development-friendly platform.

If you are looking for a platform primarily to ease the workload on your developers and to build applications with a high degree of complexity, then the criteria for evaluation would be different.

It is also noteworthy that you may decide to adopt two platforms: one to nurture your citizen development program and the other to focus on high-complexity applications to help augment faster development.

Let us expand on the key aspects to consider for either of them:

# No Code or Citizen Development Platforms:

Key factors to consider while evaluating No Code or Citizen Development Platforms:

1. Ease of Use

2. Ease of Application/Workflow Builder

3. Ease of Deployment

4. Ease of Integration

5. Ease of Maintenance

6. Availability of Governance Mechanisms

7. Depth of Access Controls through Roles & Responsibilities

8. Ease of Custom Reporting

9. Availability of Collaboration Tools within the Platform

10. Availability of Reusables Library

11. Ability to Reuse Existing Artifacts

12. Device Support

13. Vendor Support and Community

14. Pricing and Licensing Models

15. Performance and Scalability

16. Security & Compliance

17. Future Roadmap and Innovation

Let us explore them one by one:

**Ease of Use:** Citizen Development platforms are targeted at business users and predominantly are leveraged for use cases that are created and operated by business stakeholders for business teams. Hence, ease of use for creators and end users must be paramount. Business users are often frustrated with the low quotient of user experience on business applications, and they do not want another application that adds to their work and pain. Some key aspects to consider while evaluating ease of use are:

- Intuitive Interface: Allows for easy navigation, clean and well-organized layouts with clear labels and icons, and self-guiding user experience designs.

- Mobile Capabilities for End users – Must allow performing day-to-day activities in an elaborate fashion, as opposed to mere review of notifications or reports.

- Availability of contextual help and click-through guided tutorials.

- Learning Curve: Evaluate the platform's learning curve with the help of available learning materials, support, and communities.

## Ease of Application Workflow Builder:

Many factors we have explored under the ease of use heading also apply to the ease of application workflow builder, including an intuitive interface, contextual help, learning curve, etc. In addition to those, also consider:

- Availability of drag-and-drop-based tools to create forms, pages, navigations, and workflows.

- WYSIWYG: What you see is what you get editors: Many platforms would have this capability, but it is important to look for a rich set of design tools such as layout editors, form builders, theming templates, styling features, etc. Again, these must be intuitive and easy to navigate.

**Ease of Deployment:** Business users must have easy ways to test and deploy changes. This could include simplified mechanisms to simulate experiences through role impersonations and then one-click deployment mechanisms from development to test to production instances. Availability of version control and rollback mechanisms is also equally important, as easy deployment mechanisms are not useful without rollback mechanisms of a similar nature.

**Ease of Integration:** While discussing types of Low Code Platforms, we also discussed the Low Code Integration platforms that adopt the drag-and-drop approach to develop integrations between different systems. While these may be niche integration development platforms, regular No Code platforms must provide Graphical User Interface-driven, drag-and-drop-based integration tools as part of the platform to allow Business Users or citizen developers to create integrations with minimum skills.

Many platforms falter on this front and sermonize that integrations are to be only performed by IT teams. While this may be often true that integrations would still be managed by IT teams, platforms that can provide GUIs to manage integrations would have an upper hand, as this allows for fusion teams and COE-based teams to manage integrations with varied levels of skill sets.

Along with the availability of GUIs, it is also important to evaluate the integration capabilities. Availability of APIs to perform

Create, Read, Update, delete (CRUD) operations on the platform, the platform's ability to call REST/SOAP-based APIs to trigger real-time integrations, Publisher – Subscriber based integration mechanisms, scheduler-based integrations, database connectors are some key capabilities to look for.

It is also important to understand API throttle limits, if any, to have clarity on supported integration loads and compare those to probable loads expected for use cases envisaged on the platform.

## Ease of Maintenance:

- Evaluate the ease of making changes to applications, workflows, data models, and integrations post-go-live. Are the constructs flexible for modifications on the fly? Do they allow for quick-fix deployments and rollbacks? How do these changes affect downstream workflows, integrations, and data, and what mechanisms are in place to show dependencies and resolve them in a guided fashion?

- Availability of support channels is key, as citizen developers may need to reach out to platform support at different times based on work schedules. Also, the support channels must be trained to address queries of business users, rather than the usual tech support teams that assume their customers to have a high degree of technical acumen.

- Bug Fixes and Resolution SLAs and timelines: Clear guidelines on bug fix reporting and SLAs for resolution must be available.

- Frequency updates and hot fixes and their impact on the day-to-day functioning must be evaluated. Do upgrades need regression testing of existing artifacts, or are they seamlessly induced with no intervention required?

- Vendor Stability: Consider investing in a well-established platform with a track record and reference customers that can invest in maintenance and support.

- User Community and Feedback Mechanisms: The availability of user forums enables the sharing of ideas and often expands the horizon of use cases. The existence of strong and participating communities is a sign of a good platform.

## Availability of Governance Mechanisms:

Governance is a critical function for a No Code Platform. While business users are familiar with their processes and may do a better job of creating and maintaining those processes than developers, they may not be familiar with constructs of data modeling, data & information security, and integrity. Therefore, it falls on the shoulders of the IT teams to be able to ensure information security and data integrity principles of the organization are not breached.

As adoption of such platforms grows in organizations, it also becomes necessary to have a clear view of what applications and workflows are being built by whom, which ones are actively used and which ones are dormant, and who made what changes. This is key to ensuring the platform is clean and to ensure accountability.

Hence, the No Code platform under consideration must have robust governance mechanisms to cover monitoring, tracking, and controls to perform actions from a system perspective.

## Depth of Access Controls:

Role-based access controls are a basic feature for all kinds of software today. However, for Citizen Developer Platforms, additional controls are required as such platforms tend to have wider administrative or configuration access across the organization.

No Code platforms must provide role-based access controls at various levels:

- Platform Level: At the Platform level, there should be Admin access to manage users, key platform-level configurations such as user creation and access, governance module to control and monitor platform usage.

- Application level: At an application level, there must be a provision to provide users with different roles that restrict their access to processes, data, and integration exclusively. Hence, allowing for different types of users within the fusion teams to collaborate effectively as per the roles assigned to them.

- Process/Workflow Level: This is an additional layer of role-based access that restricts access to users within an application, allowing for different processes within an application to be monitored, administered, and accessed by different users.

- Data Level: Provision to control access to data based on an inheritance-based approach must allow for data access to be controlled at various points, platforms, applications, processes, sections within processes, data tables, and restricting access to specific rows/columns within the data tables based on access control rules.

## Ease of Custom Reporting:

Despite the availability of several sophisticated reporting and analytics tools in the market, easy access to analytics is a challenge for many business users even to date. This is primarily due to integration challenges in getting data in real-time to these reporting platforms.

No Code platforms must provide a simple drag-and-drop-based reporting mechanism within the platform to enable Citizen Developers to create reports, dashboards as and when required.

Below are some key features to validate:

- Availability of drag-and-drop for report and dashboard creation.

- Wide range of visualizations including bar graphs, pie charts, line graphs, scatter plots, heat maps, and others.

- Allows for full-text search, ad-hoc queries, and flexible filters to slice and dice data.

- Data export capability in different formats.

- Scheduled sharing of reports with groups of stakeholders.

## *Collaborative Tools:*

Collaboration tools have become an integral part of work post the pandemic. If your organization has already embraced collaboration for sharing ideas, content, and communication beyond the usual meetings, then you could use that instead of looking at this as a function of the platform under evaluation.

If that is not the case, then this is essential to enable a culture of collaboration among fusion teams. Scaling Citizen Development often involves establishing robust communities that share, nurture, and celebrate work, and this is only possible with a collaboration tool that is closely embedded in the work culture of the organization.

**Reusable Library:** Most platforms do provide a template library of prebuilt applications or workflows to use. If you are evaluating industry- or domain-based platforms, it may be worthwhile to perform a detailed analysis of the prebuilt applications/artifacts on the platform to assess their fit to industry- or domain-specific processes.

**Ability to Reuse:** When processes, applications, and pages are created, the platforms must provide ways to reuse them in the form of export-import capabilities. This is a critical function to increase productivity. In building large COE-based Citizen Development practices, reuse of artifacts and applications created by others goes a long way in promoting the value of such platforms and saves time.

**Device Support:** Device support is critical for all kinds of software today. Since applications and workflows, in this case, would be built by Citizen Developers, they may not really have the technical acumen to build or test for multiple devices. Hence, it is extremely important that the applications, forms, and pages built by them are systematically processed to render effectively across devices such as desktops, mobile, or tablets. Availability of whitelisted native mobile apps on iOS and Android is a must. Ability to build custom mobile apps is a nice-to-have function, as this usually requires some amount of coding and would be addressed by Low Code platforms rather than No Code platforms.

**Vendor Support & Community:** We have touched upon vendor support and the good effects of a strong user community in other headings above as well. Vendors in this space are expected to grow their product capability on a day-to-day basis as this is an evolving field; as such, it is also important to vet the vendor beyond the product capabilities as well.

- Support Model: Evaluate vendor's response times, support hours and days, and support channels provided, such as email, calls, and chat.

- SLAs and Escalation Mechanisms: Clear standards for issue classification and resolution must be established, along with escalation matrices identified.

- Training and onboarding processes must ensure simple and easy-to-access training documentation, classroom-based training programs if needed, and also role-based self-paced online learning programs.

- Detailed product documentation must be available publicly and online, and it must be regularly updated to keep up with any changes, feature releases, or bug fixes.

- Thriving User Community and Forums buzzing with posts and threads on questions and ideas always indicate a healthy customer base and avenues to explore ideas and support.

- Professional Services and Implementation Partner Ecosystems are a must even for No-Code Platforms, although they may not be at the same scale as that for ERP or CRM product lines.

- Customer References and Reviews that establish large user bases and a large number of use cases, over a prolonged period, can go a long way in establishing the credibility of vendors and platforms.

- Physical or regional presence of vendor teams would build comfort and trust. It would also help vendors to better understand regional flavors and needs.

**Pricing Models** with Low Code No Code in general could be a complicated affair. Unlike COTS, SaaS, or Infrastructure buying, No Code platform pricing models may not be straightforward. The most common pricing model for No Code Platforms would be user-based pricing. However, user-based pricing may not always work out to be economical. Vendors typically devise other pricing models that are driven by parameters such as data/process-related objects, application-related objects, number of transactions executed, etc.

If these are cloud-based models, you may further have options of a public cloud-based or private cloud-based hosting options.

It is essential to understand the pricing model well to be certain of the expected costs for the platform, both the initial investment and the recurring costs annually.

Other than the platform costs, additional costs to be evaluated would be those related to implementation and support costs.

Implementation costs must also include costs for training. If there is none, it would be wise to get it included as part of the negotiations.

**Performance & Scalability:** The performance of a No Code platform is as critical as any other business application in an organization's IT landscape. No Code platforms over a period may house several business-critical processes and applications. Therefore, it is important to evaluate the performance and scalability of the platform.

- **Concurrent Users**: Evaluate whether the platform can scale in terms of accommodating a high number of concurrent end users, as well as users who would perform development work, in line with the workforce strength of your organisation.

- **Data Size and Volumes:** Over a period, a No-Code platform would process millions of transactions and house similar volumes of master datasets such as customers, items, suppliers, employees, etc. It would process transactions with bulky attachments such as documents and other types of files. The platform in question must be able to handle the same; if there are limits to this, those must be established at the evaluation stage.

- **Platform Performance:** One must evaluate the platform response time with various devices for different actions like platform loads, saves, updates, submissions, reviews, loading and accessing reports, etc. The response times must be within the acceptable limits of the NFR (Non-Functional Requirements) guidelines of your organization.

- **Application Complexity:** Verify any limits on the creation of forms, limits to fields, limits to workflow branches, limits to the number of steps, integration call limits, API limits, etc., to ensure sufficient limits are provided for scalability.

- **Infrastructure Requirements:** If the platform you choose is on-premises, or if you need to provision cloud infrastructure for hosting the platform, then you would need to carefully evaluate various infrastructure needs. Ranging from hardware required, perform load testing to ensure load balancing, security, network, and other parameters. If this is a cloud-hosted solution managed by the vendor, you may want to perform load or performance tests or solicit third-party performance test reports to ensure adherence to your NFR needs.

**Security and Compliance:** Security evaluations, again, must be guided by the NFR requirements of the organization and any standards that one would set for business-critical applications must also be applied to No Code Platforms.

- **Compliance and Regulatory Certifications:** Platforms under evaluation must present compliance and accreditations such as ISO, SOC 1, 2, 3, HIPAA or PCI, or other industry-specific ones depending on your organization's needs, provisions for adherence to Governmental regulations such as GDPR. Ensure that the platform has features to allow you to meet any other compliance obligations that may apply based on the industry or region you operate in.

- **Role-Based Access Control:** We have already explored the importance of role-based access controls and the need for various tiered role-based access. This is sacrosanct from a security standpoint.

- **Data and Integration Security: The** Platform must provide robust mechanisms to prevent unauthorized data access and secure integration layers with secure authentication mechanisms to enable secure transmission and prevent unauthorized access.

- **Audit Logs:** Platforms must provide detailed audit logs on end-user actions as well as administration or configuration actions to have a detailed view of who did what and when. This is critical for No Code or Citizen Development Platforms as tracking user actions is necessary to allocate accountability.

- **Security Assessments:** Perform Security Assessments to ensure adherence to NFRs and also solicit third-party certifications on security and vulnerability assessments and corrective action plans for any outstanding vulnerabilities, if any.

**Future Roadmap and Innovation:** No code platforms must present a future roadmap of items in the backlog for delivery. With the ever-changing landscape of various advancements and consolidation in this space, no platform can boast of a product that is fully self-sufficient. Vendors that acknowledge the drawbacks and plan for resolution on their roadmap command more respect and trust among customers. Vendors who maintain a good feedback loop with their customers would also have the roadmap influenced by popular demand from customers, and that would also be a sign of healthy customer relations.

While the above list covers a lot of the key aspects one must consider, the list is certainly not exhaustive. In conclusion to this section, I would like to humbly suggest never choose a vendor that says yes to all your demands; rather, choose a vendor that acknowledges shortcomings or risks and provides mitigation mechanisms or action plans for resolution.

Recently, I have seen a trend where companies look for full compliance with RFPs released, and the RFPs tend to demand the earth and sky in one document.

I would also urge vendors to answer such documents as truthfully as possible without leaving room for interpretation to ensure clarity.

## Low Code Platforms:

All factors we consider while evaluating No Code platforms also apply for the evaluation of low code platforms; however, there are some additional factors to consider, which we will explore in this section:

Additional factors to consider while evaluating low code development platforms:

- Complex Omni-Channel Experiences

- Ease of Extensibility and Customization.

- DevOps Practices & CI/CD Capabilities

- Developer Independence.

**Complex Omni Channel Experiences:** Low code platforms must provide features to curate personalized, engaging, and consistent user experiences across multiple channels. Look for the below capabilities to ascertain that the platform in question could support such initiatives –

- Assess whether the platform supports multiple channels such as web, mobile, chatbots, IVRs, social media, and other channels relevant to you, such as SMS, USSD, etc., depending on industry and region. Channel support must also include capabilities such as geolocation, camera integration, and voice recognition chatbot integration.

- Platform must support responsive design so that the pages, forms, and applications built can adapt to different devices and provide the expected user experience.

- Platform must allow for cross-channel and cross-platform personalization that could be delivered on a real-time basis. This would be a key component of delivering customer-facing applications using low code platforms.

- Real-time Sync: We have already explored the different capabilities to be considered for integration in the previous section. Low code platforms must have a robust mechanism to allow for real-time data sync in massive amounts. Tech-heavy industries such as Banking, Retail, or Telecom may require heavy loads of real-time data transfer for all kinds of applications.

- A/B Testing: The platform must allow for A/B or multivariate testing to test different scenarios presented and select the right user experience journeys based on the results.

**Ease of Extensibility and Customization:** Low Code platforms, unlike no code platforms, are not restricted by drag-and-drop options alone. Low code platforms, therefore, must allow for sophisticated customization in terms of processes/workflows, user interface, integrations, and multichannel app building.

**DevOps Practices:** Low code platforms are often chosen in place of custom development of complex business-critical applications; hence, the platform in question must also align with your DevOps requirements throughout the development and deployment process. Below are some common parameters to evaluate-

- Platform must provide an easy integration mechanism with popular CI/CD tools and frameworks such as Jenkins, GitLab, etc.

- It should allow for automated build, test, and deploy of applications in different environments.

- Quality Assurance features, such as unit testing, integration testing, regression, and smoke testing, are built into the platform.

- Platform must provide robust capabilities for version control, allowing developers to track and manage changes to applications at various levels such as code, configuration, and assets.

- The platform must allow for controlled environment management, including features like cloning, automated deployments, testing, data and configuration maintenance, and purging for test and development environments. Dashboards must be available to monitor the health and usage of different environments for various parameters such as load, errors, usage, users, logins, audit logs, active integrations, applications, and workflow usage metrics.

- Platform must support containerization technologies and container orchestration frameworks.

## Developer independence:

- Developers should have the space to generate customized code wherever necessary for UI, Workflows, Data models, Processes, Applications, or integration and plug them in appropriately.

- Reusability of code or components already built must be easy and seamless to allow developers to assimilate code built by them previously, others in the organization, or developers from a larger community of users of the platform around the world.

- Open standards-based coding standards and frameworks should be supported so that developers can leverage their existing skills or easily brush up and upskill if needed. Avoid choosing platforms with proprietary languages or frameworks.

Although we have discussed in detail the various evaluation parameters for No Code and low code platforms, the question of which platform to choose for your needs may not yet be fully clear.

Many senior stakeholders are often in a dilemma over the choices that are available in the market and generally go with the cheaper options to lower financial risks in case of failure.

A better and safer way to lower risk and also to distribute accountability would be to involve key stakeholders in the evaluation process. If you are looking for a citizen development platform, it may not be a bad idea to involve the business teams, get them access to the platform, and allow them to build a prototype.

Unlike traditional development, these platforms must be easy to learn and adopt, and therefore the time spent would be considerably lower. This will help in the easy acceptability and transition of business and IT teams on such platforms. Any platform that is difficult to learn and does not fit into a prototyping model can safely be assumed to be too complicated for a citizen development or No Code model.

Low Code Platform evaluations might be still more difficult to navigate, but the same rules apply; only here the developers are your stakeholders. Do they find it easy to navigate, build, test, and deploy? That is the question one should ask.

Therefore, in either evaluation, a Proof of Concept or Prototyping phase, that activity engages end users from your organization should be a key evaluation criterion.

Evaluation of Low Code, No Code platforms is often tricky with several internal as well as external considerations. As you expand the scope of your evaluation and vet the needs, it is possible that you will find that one platform may not fit your needs completely.

While it is always easier to rely on the requirement at hand and the budget provisioned for the same, it may be worthwhile conducting platform evaluations not based on 1-2 use cases, but with a more long-term approach.

This would help set in motion a strategy for automation that is sustainable in the long run, paving the way for efficient maintenance, reduced integration complexity, and easier adoption.

Depending on the specific needs and the nature and vision of your organization, the type and number of platforms you choose may differ.

I have come across organizations with a clear vision for citizen development opting for two platforms – one to manage their Citizen Development initiatives and the other, a robust Low Code Platform to help their developers.

In other cases, where organizations have clearly set aside citizen development initiatives, they prefer to go with a low code platform alone.

In more specialized cases, I have seen customers have a Low Code Platform but opt to choose low code platforms for domain- or industry-related use cases where the platforms have prebuilt templates aligned to the domain or industry.

Therefore, IT and Digital Transformation leaders need not shy away from choosing more than one platform for their Digital Transformation initiatives. Choose wisely based on your own needs; there is no best practice or industry norm regarding the number of Low Code No Code platforms an organization could have.

# Chapter 4

# Organizational Alignment

*Large organizations are like dinosaurs—strong and enduring, but to survive and thrive, they must learn to dance with agility and grace.*

Once you have chosen a Low Code Platform, the next steps of assimilation, build, testing, go live, adoption, and continuous improvement would fit very well into your organization's existing time-tested Project/Product Management approach, irrespective of whether your organization follows Waterfall or Agile.

Although agile models may be much more well-suited for low code platforms than traditional Pro-Code based development.

However, No Code or Citizen Development platforms may need extra care. The induction of such platforms into an ecosystem that is not accustomed to such practices may be challenging in many ways. Therefore, it is important to establish organizational alignment throughout the journey, starting from the evaluation stage.

Below are some key factors to consider:

## Understanding Resistance to Change:

Citizen Development platforms may face a higher degree of resistance than other platforms or applications in general. While, on the one hand, they may ease the process of creating applications and tremendously reduce time to market and improve efficiencies, they also require a significant change in mindset and working styles.

IT departments may fear that their job is at risk, as business teams would now be capable of making their own changes or apps without contacting IT. Business teams may be worried that this would increase the burden of work on them.

Overcoming resistance to change requires a thoughtful and strategic approach. Below are some means and ways to be prepared and plan to effect change, particularly for Citizen Development/ low code platform adoption:

## Create a sense of shared ownership:

- Identify those stakeholders that are impacted by the project or its outcomes.

- Engage them and address their concerns.

- Make them an active part of the project by giving them the importance that is due. Ensure their inputs are considered and accounted for appropriately.

## Empower early adopters and promoters:

Irrespective of their position and level in the organization, early adopters and promoters must be encouraged and empowered. Good feedback and word of mouth on the ground can create a positive environment about the project and allow for more end users or employees to view it affirmatively.

## Identify Detractors:

Like you identify promoters, it is also necessary to identify detractors with high stakes and visibility. Ensure their concerns are addressed, and they are on board.

When detractors are engaged early and empowered, they often become change ambassadors.

# Engage stakeholders regularly:

- Set up separate engagements for different stakeholder groups to communicate progress and receive feedback and inputs at regular intervals.

- Allow them to experience key milestones as their own and be excited about feature releases.

- Reward stakeholders who are early adopters.

# Provide Training and Support:

- Give users the skills for success in a citizen development/low-code environment. Offer comprehensive training programs that cater to different learning styles, stakeholder groups, and levels of expertise.

- Provide ongoing support through help desks, peer mentoring, accessible documentation, and FAQs.

# Address Cultural Concerns:

- Align the values of citizen development with the existing culture of the organization. This may require careful consideration of the operating model and governance structures.

- Encourage a mindset that views change as an opportunity rather than a threat.

# Monitor and adapt:

- Highlight the value of new applications built through sessions and roadshows, focusing on how the applications address end-user needs and ease of use.

- Continuously monitor the progress of the citizen development initiative and be open to feedback. Adjust your approach as needed to address emerging challenges and reinforce the positive aspects of the change.

- Celebrate milestones and acknowledge the contributions of those who are driving the change.

## Stakeholders:

We often refer to stakeholders in this book, and it is probably also good to understand how to identify key stakeholders:

Typically, look for the below groups of people who are expected to play key roles in any project:

- **Business line leads and Managers:** These are department heads, business unit or entity heads, or direct reports. They are highly influential and key stakeholders for any project with a business impact/outcome.

- **Subject Matter Experts:** Could be either from the Business or IT organisation. These are people with excellent knowledge or understanding of the domain or the processes of their domains or departments. Their input would be critical to any project's success.

- **Customers:** Could be both internal customers or externals. They are the most important stakeholders in any project. They will be the end users of your application and usually the ones who fund the project or would pay for the output in one way or another.

- **Vendors:** These are companies that provide key resources for the project, which could be software, tools, infrastructure, or people. You are their customer, but you are also dependent on them to get your work completed on time. A delay from them could adversely impact your plan.

- **Government and Regulators:** These are external stakeholders that, on most occasions, do not get involved in your project directly. However, their policies may have an impact on your project or its goals. Keep a close watch on any decisions that may impact the project or its goals and track them through a risk register.

- **Executive leadership:** This is the top management of the company. They are the most important stakeholders, and their trust and buy-in secure the project. They do not get involved in the project's day-to-day affairs but are interested in its outcomes and how it can add value to the company's strategic objectives.

- **Key Users and User Acceptance Testers/Beta Testers:** These are the small select set of end users that get to see and test your work firsthand. Their feedback is crucial as their experience would be the same as the larger end-user community.

You have to deal with each of these stakeholder groups differently at different times.

The stakeholder power matrix is a tool that can help plot how you must deal with the different groups and how to segregate them.

Below is the stakeholder power matrix:

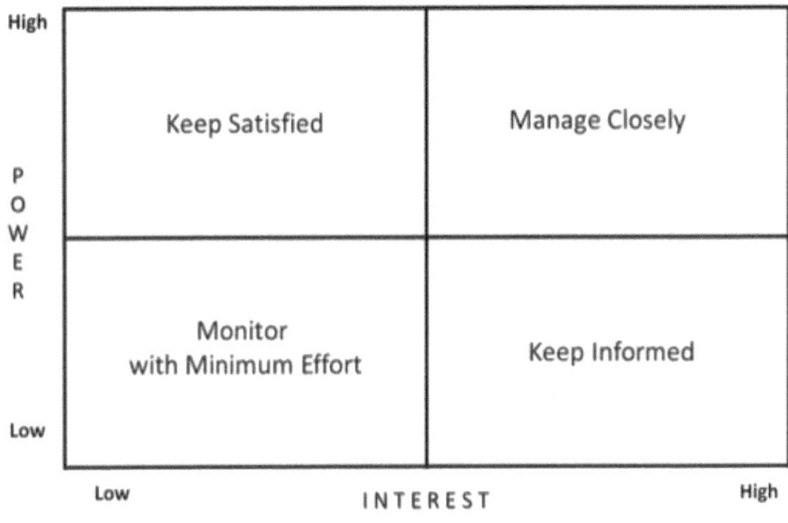


*Fig 4.1*

# The four quadrants are:

**High Power High Interest**: These stakeholders are decision-makers and have the biggest impact on the project's success. You would do well to keep them always on your side and happy.

**High Power Low Interest**: These are stakeholders that have low interest now, but they wield high power, so monitor them closely and keep them informed of the progress always.

**Low Power High Interest:** Keep them adequately informed and ensure there are no major issues arising with this group. They are usually the lower management or end users who could be impacted by the project, and noise from them may pique the interest of the high-power stakeholders.

**Low Power Low Interest:** Monitor them and provide them with minimal updates, such as newsletters or monthly updates.

# Improve Governance:

Citizen development enables people close to business processes to create custom solutions, leading to faster innovation and more engaged employees. However, it can result in unauthorized applications, security vulnerabilities, and integration challenges without proper oversight. Balancing innovation and control is crucial.

We will explore the operating model in further detail in a different chapter, as it is a topic that needs focus.

In this chapter, we will limit ourselves to looking at governance from an IT perspective and how that works with low code or Citizen Development Projects.

In organizations where the business introduces Citizen development, there might be a lack of trust and bad blood between business and IT. Business teams might feel that IT is not delivering on its tasks, and IT might see the introduction of such platforms as a threat to security.

IT would view such platforms as shadow IT.

In other cases, IT might be on board with the concept but worried about compliance and security risks.

In either scenario, a strong governance structure becomes the need of the hour.

IT can design its governance around the following pillars to ensure applications built using low code or citizen development platforms are compliant and do not breach security principles.

- Design Authority: Is a committee or process with a board to review and approve application design. The design authority may also set guidelines to be followed for any new application design.

- Data Models: Data is precious. Ensuring data is collected securely and maintaining data quality is paramount. Hence, IT can also define data modeling standards that prescribe how data is handled and moved within and out of low code and citizen development platforms in use.

- Security Policy: Security in terms of authorisation and authentication, access, roles, and responsibilities at various levels, Application level, Process level, and Data level need to be defined and must be adhered to by all projects, including those delivered by Citizen Developers.

- IT Risks: Primarily driven by NFRs, the IT risks cover any resources and infrastructure requirements needed by the platforms to operate, including space, load, integration throughputs, etc. These have to be explored during the initial suitability assessments to ensure no requirements go overboard with their needs that could potentially strain the infrastructure.

Irrespective of how free the operating model is, IT security must always be with the IT organization.

## Establish ROI:

Establishing ROI through various metrics to present the value delivered by such projects and platforms is key.

We look at establishing value and the outcome of projects in another chapter later in the book.

However, it is also important to measure the effectiveness of the project or the Citizen Development Program itself.

It is important to understand the following:

- Are we effectively allocating time and resources to such projects?

- Is the organization adapting and benefiting from such initiatives?

- Are individuals sufficiently skilled and trained?

- Are the developers overloaded, or do they have enough work?

- Do we have any intra- or inter-departmental collaboration issues?

To achieve this, we must have governance, an operating model, and a way of establishing value in place.

## Allocate Accountability:

Fostering a sense of accountability in the organization is critical for the success of low code projects and for building citizen development programs.

Having accountability in projects brings clarity and aligns objectives of the project and organization with that of the employees.

Below are some key considerations for having accountability engraved in the culture of the organization:

- Establishing Clear Roles and Responsibilities: This is one of the foundational elements for any project that you may run. Roles must be clear to all stakeholders and team members involved.

- Allow for the teams to make mistakes and learn from them. While accountability means taking ownership of mistakes, it is very important to allow the teams a level of freedom to learn. That means people will make mistakes and learn from them.

Do not use accountability parameters to blame people. Rather, it is an instrument to track and learn from the mistakes, to avoid repeating them in the future.

- Create transparency in the organization about success, failure, and delays. Transparency at all levels ensures an increase in trust across the organization. All stakeholders and team members would feel free to voice out concerns and accept mistakes. This leads to a sense of increased ownership.

- Recognise and Reward success. Appreciate citizen developers and other contributors for achieving milestones.

A common way to assess and track accountability and responsibility is the **RACI matrix.**

Below is an example of a simple RACI matrix; this can be developed further based on your organization's practices.

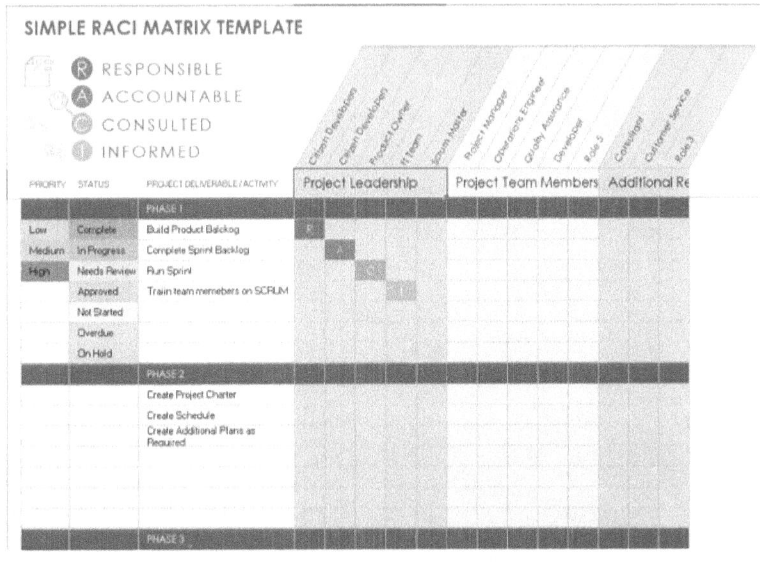



*Fig 4.2*

The RACI matrix indicates Responsible, Accountable, Consulted, and Informed:

**Responsible** is the person who performs the task; this could be assigned to more than one person per task.

**Accountable:** This person delegates the work and reviews it before it is deemed completed. You would normally have only one Accountable person per task.

**Consulted:** One or more persons could be consulted on any given task. These people provide their input and advice, which may be key to the completion of the task. They are not responsible for the completion of the task.

**Informed:** These are one or more persons, usually stakeholders, who need to be informed or kept in the loop with the progress or completion of tasks.

# Identifying CD Projects

*The power of assessment lies in its ability to reveal not just what is, but what can be.*

# Fitment Assessment:

A fitment assessment is essential for determining whether a proposed Citizen Development Project aligns with organizational goals and technological capabilities. This process involves evaluating the project's objectives, scope, and alignment with the strategic priorities of the organization.

## Key Steps in a Fitment Assessment:

**Objective Alignment:** Assess whether the project aligns with the organization's strategic objectives. Projects that support core business functions or strategic initiatives are more likely to be successful.

**Technical Feasibility:** Evaluate the technical requirements and compatibility with existing systems. Citizen development tools often offer flexibility, but they must integrate seamlessly with the current IT infrastructure. Citizen development platforms may not be suitable for all kinds of technical requirements as the flexibility of building with no code or low code could impose technical restrictions.

**Resource Availability:** Analyse the availability of resources, including skilled personnel and budget. Citizen development projects should be feasible given the organization's resource constraints.

**Risk Assessment:** Identify potential risks associated with the project, including security concerns, compliance issues, and potential impacts on existing systems.

A thorough fitment assessment ensures that Citizen Development projects are not only viable but also strategically beneficial.

Below is a reference from PMI of a fitment through a scorecard method to assess if a project is a viable Citizen Development Project. This is a good example of conducting project complexity and suitability assessment. You may follow similar assessments based on your organization's character and needs.

| Statement | Not at All (# - 0) | Some what (# - 1) | Very Much (# - 2) |
|---|---|---|---|
| This solution requires little to no custom coding. | | | |
| The cost of this solution is favorable in comparison with alternatives. | | | |
| This solution will require regular and/or quick customization. | | | |
| There are capacity constraints within the IT team preventing them from delivering this solution in the required timeframe. | | | |

| Statement | Not at All<br><br>(# - 0) | Some what<br><br>(# - 1) | Very Much<br><br>(# - 2) |
|---|---|---|---|
| Our team is open to learning and using citizen development application platforms. | | | |
| The citizen development approach is less disruptive to the customer. | | | |
| Using citizen development matches the strategic direction of the organization. | | | |
| Total = | | | |

*Fig. 5.1: Reference: PMI Citizen Developer:*

## Project Requirements:

**Functional Requirements:** These define the specific needs and objectives of the business, such as improving customer service or streamlining internal processes. Business requirements focus on what the solution should achieve in terms of functionality and performance.

The Functional Requirements should typically describe the following:

- What should the application be able to do?

- How should the application function?

- What features are needed in the application?

- What processes would be run in the application?

- What data would go as inputs to the processes in the application, and what data would be generated as output?

- Who can have access to the input and output data, and how would access be provided, and at what steps?

- How will the application operate?

**Non-Functional Requirements:** These encompass the quality attributes that the system must possess, such as performance, scalability, and security. NFRs define how the system performs its functions rather than what it does.

Ensure that NFRs are considered alongside business requirements to deliver a solution that meets both functional and quality expectations. For instance, while a business requirement might dictate a new feature, an NFR might specify how quickly that feature should respond under load.

Impact on Citizen Development: Citizen developers must understand both types of requirements to build solutions that not only meet business needs but also adhere to technical standards and constraints.

Balancing NFRs with business requirements ensures that Citizen Development projects are both effective and robust.

NFRs must cater to the two forms of requirements:

**Regulatory and Compliance-Related Requirements:** These could be requirements mandated by the territories or industries the company operates in or could also be requirements mandated internally by the company for effective adherence to security and architectural principles.

**Quality Requirements:** These sets of requirements describe application attributes related to quality, such as page load speed, integration throughputs, accessibility, browsers and devices, scalability, availability, performance, disaster recovery, etc.

Who should be involved in collecting requirements?

Based on the requirements and the fitment/suitability assessments, one must determine the type of project that one is about to embark on.

## IT Owned:

Projects with requirements that demand a high degree of integration are more UI-driven or have a high degree of customization requirements are typically best handled by the IT organization.

Such projects should involve business teams at various stages to provide inputs, review if requirements are met, and participate in testing and training.

However, the overall ownership of these projects remains with the IT organization. The tools used in such projects typically involve high code-driven platforms, which may have integrations with low code or citizen development apps.

## IT-Led:

The second type of projects would be classified as IT-led. These projects typically involve some level of customization or integration. However, they could also potentially have a significant portion of deliverables that could be built using low code platforms or citizen development platforms.

Such projects would involve active participation from business teams and citizen developers, not only in the requirement gathering, testing, and training phases, but also in actively building applications through low code or no code apps.

## IT Aided:

The third type of projects is the ones with low integration or customization requirements. Such projects are ideal Citizen Development projects and may be fully owned by Citizen development teams or business teams. Do not forget your IT teams on such projects, as their contribution is still imperative.

IT teams would take a back seat to allow business to own and drive these projects, but critical oversight, especially related to security and architectural policy adherence, is a must.

Now that you have identified the projects, let's get down to project execution.

# Chapter 6

# Executing CD Projects

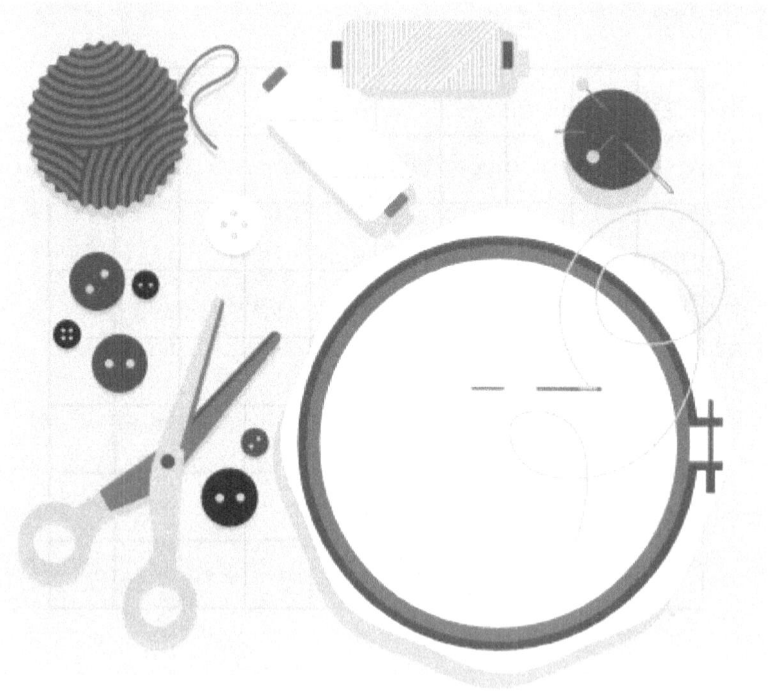

*In any project, every step is a stitch in a grand design,*
*and the outcome is a work of art.*

Executing Citizen Development projects needs its own set of processes. Running it as a project is always a good idea to keep track of progress, risks, and issues and to ensure timely completion. No matter which teams own it and how simple the application is, without a process and plan in place, successful completion would be a challenge.

But Citizen Development projects cannot have very stringent project methodologies applied, as citizen developers are not your typical developer folk who have grown up in organizations with all these processes day in and day out. These are business folks with other work or priorities who do not have exposure to such in-depth project methodologies.

It is important to devise a lean project method that can drive business teams to success and yet not overburden them.

**Agile Approach** Would be best suited in this case, and we would do well to adopt only those processes and tools that are necessary at the bare minimum.

Below are some terms and tools commonly used with Scrum that I recommend using. However, please feel free to customize the approach here based on your organization's needs and complexities.

**Product Backlog**: An ordered list of all requirements needed and identified for the application being developed.

If your teams are collocated in one place while they spend time on the project, then this is best placed on a board, where they are always visible.

If your teams work remotely, then any digital tools such as Jira or other backlog tools, or spreadsheets could help with making sure the requirements are easily accessible and trackable.

**Sprint Planning**: Sprint planning is a session that initiates the Sprint and determines the requirements that are to be delivered during the Sprint. Determining what is to be delivered should be collaborative work, and all Citizen Developers must actively contribute and participate to ensure they commit to the sprint requirements and timelines based on their availability and skills.

**Sprint Backlog**: Once the sprint planning is completed, we have a subset of the Product backlog called the Sprint backlog that determines the requirements for the Sprint.

**Sprint**: A sprint is a fixed period of work that typically lasts one month or less to create consistency and ensure short iterations of delivery and feedback. For Citizen Development projects, it is recommended that we follow sprints of 1 or 2 weeks, as we expect easier development and faster delivery.

**Daily Reviews:** Daily 15-minute review meetings to check what work was done and what work is planned for the following day. Also, to discuss any risks or challenges that the team foresees or encounters.

It is highly advisable to keep the meetings short and within the 15-minute window and to take any topics that could take longer outside of this meeting to be discussed separately.

**Sprint Review:** At the end of the sprint, a quick review is conducted to see what was accomplished during the sprint. Adjust the product backlog to meet new requirements that may have come up. The session may also be used to include feedback on what went well and what could have been improved to be included in the following sprint.

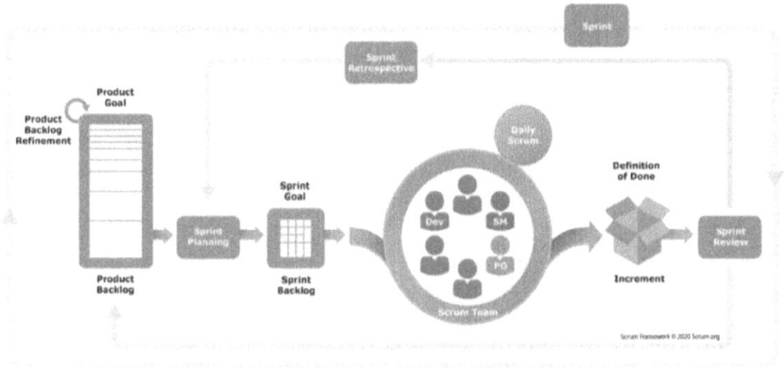



*Fig. 6.1; Reference: SCRUM.org*

Above is a reference from Scrum.org on the Agile Scrum Delivery Model.

One of the most important concepts in Scrum is the definition of Done:

The Definition of Done is a formal description of the state of the Increment when it meets the quality measures required for the product.

The moment a Product Backlog item meets the Definition of Done, an Increment is born.

The Definition of Done creates transparency by providing everyone with a shared understanding of what work was completed as part of the Increment. If a Product Backlog item does not meet the Definition of Done, it cannot be released or even presented at the Sprint Review. Instead, it returns to the Product Backlog for future consideration.

Now that we have seen key processes and tools, let's also quickly look at roles:

Again, here we would like to keep it simple and to a bare minimum. Please include additional roles that may be necessary as per your organization's needs and policies.

Product Owner: The product owner would be responsible for delivering and maximizing the value of the product/application.

The Product Owner is also accountable for effective Product Backlog management, which includes:

- Developing and explicitly communicating the Product Goal;

- Creating and clearly communicating Product Backlog items;

- Ordering Product Backlog items; and,

- Ensuring that the Product Backlog is transparent, visible, and understood.

Scrum Master: The Scrum Master is responsible for the effectiveness of the team. He is a servant leader, responsible for helping everyone understand the processes and tools, and aiding in the success of the project.

The Scrum Master serves the Scrum Team in several ways, including:

- Coaching the team members in self-management and cross-functionality;

- Helping the Scrum Team focus on creating high-value Increments that meet the Definition of Done;

- Causing the removal of impediments to the Scrum Team's progress; and,

- Ensuring that all Scrum events take place and are positive, productive, and kept within the timebox.

Citizen Developers: These are the developers who would use the citizen development tools or platforms to build applications based on the requirements.

The specific skills needed by the developers would include the ability to build applications or processes using the Citizen development platform identified, the ability to think in design terms with a focus on process flow, data flow, roles, and access.

Citizen Developers would divide various tasks for building, testing, and training among themselves based on skills and preferences within the project, based on internal discussions and mutual agreement.

- The developers are always accountable for:

- Creating a plan for the Sprint, the Sprint Backlog;

- Instilling quality by adhering to a Definition of Done;

- Adapting their plan each day towards the Sprint Goal; and,

- Holding each other accountable as professionals.

This framework is quite effective in delivering Citizen Development projects fully. Additional tools may be included, but it is key that the citizen developers are not overburdened with the process and are able to execute their tasks as smoothly as possible.

# Chapter 7

# Executing Low Code Project

While Citizen Development Project execution demands lean processes, the same may not be true with low code applications, which may stretch the complexity limits in comparison to a Citizen Development Project.

This also means that along with citizen developers, who are trained or cross-skilled business users, you may also need traditional developers.

This makes project execution and delivery slightly more complex at two levels.

One issue is that the parts of the application driven by low code components need higher governance, checks, and balances, testing, and controlled release mechanisms.

Second, the varied team member profiles mean carefully crafted mechanisms are needed to ensure compliance for coders but keep the business or citizen developers immune from the added processes and checks.

Many low code platforms themselves provide this segregation on their platforms that may help ease this variation. The no code-driven tools on the platform may allow launching and activating changes with fewer checks, whereas the low code tools on the same platform would have a much more stringent release mechanism, features that enable versioning, merging code, and rolling back changes.

This differentiation automatically allows for such tasks to be included in the planning and processes.

A low code application development may follow either SDLC or Agile forms of development depending on your organization's structure, practices, and policies.

However, I would still recommend adopting agile methods for low code projects in any organization, as it allows earlier value realization and faster delivery, which are also key reasons for the evolution of low-code platforms. You are free to choose different agile methods such as Scrum, Kanban, or XP based on the type of projects and requirements you face.

I would strongly recommend the Agile Practice Guide from PMP to review which methods would best fit your project.

You may also decide to blend different methods in order to arrive at a blended approach that best fits your project and organization's needs:

As an example of tailoring agile frameworks, one of the most common blends in widespread use involves a coordinated use of the Scrum framework, Kanban Method, and elements of the eXtreme Programming (XP) method.

Scrum provides guidance on the use of a product backlog, a product owner, a Scrum Master, and a cross-functional development team, including sprint planning, daily Scrum, sprint review, and sprint retrospective sessions as illustrated in the above chapter on project methods for Citizen Development projects. A Kanban board helps the team to further improve its effectiveness by

Visualizing the flow of work, making impediments easily visible, and allowing flow to be managed by adjusting work-in-process limits. Adding XP-inspired engineering practices such as the use of story cards, continuous integration, refactoring, automated testing, and test-driven development further increase the effectiveness of the agile team.

Below is a table from the PMP Agile guide that provides tailoring options based on project factors.

| Project Factor | Tailoring Options |
| --- | --- |
| Demand pattern: steady or sporadic. | Many teams find that using a cadence in the<br><br>(form of a regular timebox) helps them demo-retrospect and take in new work. In addition, some teams need more flexibility in their acceptance of more work. Teams can use flow-based agile with a cadence to get the best of both worlds. |
| Rate of process improvement required by the<br><br>Level of team experience | Retrospect more often and seek improvements. |

| Project Factor | Tailoring Options |
| --- | --- |
| The flow of work is often interrupted by various delays or impediments. | Consider making work visible using Kanban boards and experimenting with limits for the various areas of the work process in order to improve flow. |
| The quality of the product increments is poor. | Consider using the various test-driven development practices. This mistake-proofing discipline makes it difficult for defects to remain undetected. |
| More than one team is needed to build a product. | To scale from one to several agile teams with minimal disruption, first learn about agile program management or formal scaling. frameworks. Then, craft an approach that fits the project context. |
| The project team members are inexperienced in the use of agile approaches. | Consider starting by training team members in the fundamentals of the agile mindset principles. If the team decides to use a specific approach, such as Scrum or Kanban, provide a workshop on that approach so the team members can learn how to use it. |

*Table 7.1: Reference PMI Agile Guide*

An iterative delivery approach with low code platforms must also incorporate execution practices that help the team to track changes and release value faster. The following are some technical practices that may help in this regard:

Continuous Integration: Incorporate work frequently into the product and then retest the entire product to determine that it works. This requires CI/CD tools that make integration of incremental code easier and provide regression testing to be incorporated.

Testing at Different Levels: Unit testing to test individual functional blocks or other logically distributed blocks. End-to-End testing to test complete process flows across modules. Integration testing to ensure links between systems and applications still function as they used to before new changes were introduced. Smoke testing or sample testing with random samples may also be useful methods.

Acceptance Criteria incorporated as part of the definition of Done: This ensures that critical testing is incorporated as part of the Sprint delivery and comprehensive testing is performed before a cataloged item is accepted as "Done".

Automated Testing is incorporated to ensure mistake-proof products and incremental additions.

Frequent Demonstrations during Sprints: For all increments, schedule frequent demonstrations with end users and business users to ensure delivery of functionality is in alignment with business needs. All feedback and changes must be carefully reviewed by the product owner along with the team to incorporate them into the product backlog and then subsequently into sprint backlogs based on the consensus.

Despite these tools, it is possible that your projects may run into unforeseen roadblocks or challenges. Below are some recommended troubleshooting possibilities recommended by PMI in their Agile Practice Guide that I find very useful, along with some from my own experience.

| Pain Point | Troubleshooting Mechanisms |
|---|---|
| Unclear purpose or mission for the team. | Agile chartering for purpose – vision, mission, and mission tests |
| Unclear requirements | Help sponsors and stakeholders craft a product vision. Consider building a product roadmap using specification by example, user story mapping, and impact mapping. Bring the team and product owner together to clarify the expectations and value of a requirement. Progressively decompose the roadmap into a backlog of smaller, concrete requirements. |
| Poor user experience. | User experience design practices included in the development team involves users early and often. |
| Inaccurate estimation | Reduce the story size by splitting stories. Use relative estimation with the entire team to estimate. Consider agile modeling or spiking to understand what the story is. |

| Pain Point | Troubleshooting Mechanisms |
| --- | --- |
| Team struggles with obstacles. | A servant leader like a Scrum Master can help clear these obstacles. If the team doesn't know the options they have, consider a coach. Sometimes, the team needs to escalate stories that the team or servant leader has not been able to remove. |
| Team struggles with Skill Issues | Training on a low-code platform in use, along with material that can help them understand reusable templates and code snippets that could potentially simplify work. |
| Siloed teams, instead of cross-functional teams | Ask the people who are part of projects to self-organize as cross-functional teams. Use servant leadership skills to help the managers understand why agile needs cross-functional teams. |

*Table 7.2: Reference PMI Agile Guide*

Obviously, this section is not a complete Agile Guide and does not intend to be one. There is no right or wrong method when delivering a low-code project using Agile approaches. I would strongly recommend PMI's Agile Practice Guide for further guidance on agile methods and practices.

You must consider your project's requirements, team composition, organization's structure, and policies carefully while evaluating the right approach, frameworks, and tools for your project execution.

While a low-code project delivery would involve more nuanced methods, tools, and frameworks, that does not take away from a key principle; that is to ensure that processes are lean and do not overburden the team, but only aid them in performing work, promoting innovation, and delivering value faster.

# Chapter 8

# Stages of Building A CD Practice

*Building a CD practice is like growing a tree; the smallest beginnings can lead to great achievements.*

Building a Citizen Development Practice is a continuous process. While getting a platform and getting the first simple application done might be an easy exercise, continuing to use the platform to build more such applications and fostering a culture of citizen development could take many months if not years.

Therefore, it is key to understand the various stages in the journey of enabling Citizen Development in any organization. We will explore the various stages and also look at some key characteristics of each stage.

## First Contact:

This is the first time you start with a Citizen Development use case at your company. Typically, this starts with a specific one-off problem that needs resolution, and a low-code platform or Citizen Development platform is proposed.

At this stage, this is not really a Citizen Development practice of any kind yet. There are no governance mechanisms or accountability frameworks.

Key Characteristics at this stage:

- Project teams are either self-appointed or have no formal structure.

- Requirements are specific to a department or a use case or pain point that needs a speedy solution/resolution.

- IT involvement is minimal.

- No operating model or internal structure is available.

- Communication and stakeholder management are performed in a very ad hoc manner.

Even if the project is successful and the application is live, if the platform is left unattended, then this could become the very problem it set out to solve – Shadow IT. Yes, a low-code or citizen development platform serving only one or two use cases and without proper integration and governance structures eventually becomes another shadow IT product in the large portfolio of products.

Nevertheless, this is a very important first step in the Citizen Development journey of any organization as employees and management have experienced a Citizen Development concept for the first time.

Do the following steps to capitalize on the success:

- Recognise the success of the project and appreciate the team members within the wider organisation.

- Run a lessons-learned session to identify what went well and what could have been improved.

- Use the feedback to create basic processes and operating models for evaluation and execution of another project on the platform.

- Familiarise the larger organisation with the capabilities of the platform and other possible use cases.

- Collate requests and build a backlog of requirements/projects.

- Organize Maintenance and Support for the application built.

- Demonstrate value by measuring ROI and key metrics.

# Controlled Expansion:

This is stage 2 of your citizen development journey. At this stage, one must look at ways to increase interest and usage of the platform in a controlled manner.

Allow more Citizen Development projects and teams to function in a controlled fashion where the risk of complexity and costs is limited.

A few more successful go-lives would ensure and increase trust in the idea that Citizen Development can create value for the organization.

The following strategies may help during this stage:

- Prioritize the backlog of projects and put the low-risk, high-reward ones highest on the list for execution.

- Set up a training programme for Citizen Developers and allow interested employees to participate.

- Address governance and operating model gaps.

- Define roles and responsibilities, set accountability for products and applications developed on the platform.

- Establish communication practices.

- Engage top management and obtain their sponsorship.

- Demonstrate the value of the applications created on the platform.

- Do not forget to appreciate and recognize the good work done by citizen developers and teams, as appreciation motivates them and also others in the organization to embrace the change.

# Key roles to look at for the overall practice.

We have already explored Product Owners, CD Scrum Masters, and Citizen Developers. In addition, having a part-time role for a Community Manager who looks at CD-related communications and also manages community requests, and moderation would be key.

PMI also identifies a role for a Citizen Development Business Architect, who is responsible for overseeing and performing key strategies toward the expansion and establishment of Citizen development practice.

# Embrace:

We reach this stage when a few projects have already been successfully delivered. The top management is convinced about the value of the platform and is ready to sponsor and invest in the growth of the practice.

The idea now is to increase adoption throughout the organization to enable as many employees as possible and deliver more projects.

During this stage, use the below strategies to improve adoption:

- Establish a Project Implementation Approach or methodology.

- Revise and upgrade the operating model and governance structures.

- Formalise training programs into the HR portfolio to allow them to be accessed by a wider audience.

- Incorporate Citizen Development into the organisation's strategy.

- Increase community engagement through the establishment of a community tool within the organisation.

- Build a repository of reusable applications, templates, and code snippets from the work done so far..

- Increase IT involvement by introducing key aspects necessary for expansion such as NFR, architecture and security policies, and review mechanisms.

- Establish a joint delivery model with IT and Citizen Development teams.

- Continue to monitor project success and measure metrics and performance.

- Strengthen the community structures and promote a Citizen Development culture.

Use the fitment and suitability analysis tools set up based on the earlier chapters to identify, classify, and deliver projects.

## Scaling:

This phase occurs when citizen development has been adopted fully in your organization. You have many citizen developers and numerous projects running on the platform. Top management is fully convinced and behind this as a strategic initiative.

The idea is to standardize and stabilize processes, operating models, and frameworks put in place so far during this phase.

Use the following strategies to effectively navigate this phase:

- Work on standardisation of project methodologies

- Set up operating models – choose either the Centre of Excellence model or the Communities of Practice model.

- Inspire the communities, increase engagement, and promote and reward participation in the community.

- Implement clear accountability and responsibility structures. Owners of applications should be responsible and accountable. Determine what happens in case an owner leaves or is absent, etc.

- Governance structures in place must promote citizen development practices across the organization.

- Governance measures must be in place to review the use of the platform, harness reusables, remove or archive unused applications, and optimize usage and platform resources..

- Instil reviews and audits to ensure quality, usage, and security principles are followed.

It is now time to try large-scale transformation projects with a wider scope and usage across the organization on the platform.

## Self-Sustaining:

This is the final stage in maturity, and at this stage, the citizen development initiative would have become a significant value multiplier for the organization.

At this stage, you can boldly create a dedicated organization around Citizen Development, for various pillars such as:

- Project Management.

- Citizen developers.

- Community Moderators.

- Trainers.

- Citizen Development Business Architects.

These roles could further nurture and grow the organization. At this stage, it is important to put in place a constant review and feedback mechanism for all processes and frameworks.

Use the feedback to continuously revise and improve the models and inculcate a strong culture of citizen development. Continue to follow the key strategies highlighted in the previous stages.

# Chapter 9

# Establishing Value

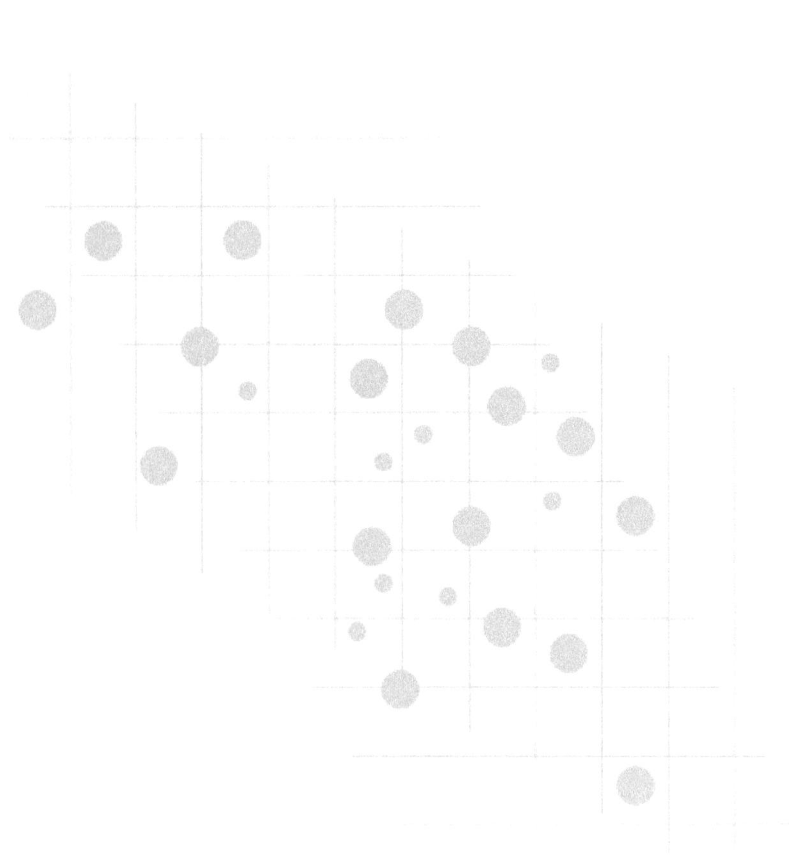

*You cannot manage what you don't measure.*

Establishing the value of low code/Citizen Development projects in an organization is of utmost importance.

Typically, Enterprise applications are divided into various conventional pillars such as ERP, HCM, Supply chain, CRM, ITSM, etc. These are now widely accepted throughout the world as mandatory.

Low-Code or Citizen Development Platforms, on the other hand, do not start with a preset objective and must be adopted by organizations based on their own needs and priorities.

Under such circumstances, it becomes critical that value from such projects or platforms is rigorously measured, tracked, and reported. Without such measures, the platforms run the risk of falling by the wayside and eventually being shelved.

Below are some of the most important factors to help determine the value of your low-code/Citizen Development platforms.

## Time to Market:

One of the main pain points of traditional development and projects was the time taken for anything to start delivering value. Usually, this is a few months post-go live or post-launch when the application built starts achieving its set objectives.

This was also one of the prime reasons for the advent of low-code and citizen development platforms.

Therefore, time to market or time to value, is a factor to be measured and reported.

Consider the following:

- **Time to go live/launch:** Time taken for the project to reach its milestone where end users have begun using the application or platform.

- **Time to learn and expand:** Time taken to train end users or developers on the platform for future projects. This must be low compared to traditional implementation; if not, it means that there is not much use of the platform or using low code as an approach.

- **Backlog Clearance Acceleration:** Low-code or Citizen development platforms must help deliver more projects faster and with less time to learn and scale, which means that the projects in the backlog must be picked up for work and completed at a significantly higher pace.

## Revenue Levers:

Projects that can show a contribution to an increase in revenue are most appreciated in organizations. Having said that, not all projects may actively contribute to revenue levers. If that is the case with your projects, then refrain from force-fitting revenue metrics into your ROI measurements. That will only dent the credibility of the platform or projects in question. Instead, focus on other levers.

If you genuinely do see revenue attribution, then project it with clear metrics. Below are some to consider:

- Incremental Sales Attribution: This must be clearly laid out in terms of metrics such as an increase in leads, orders, and sales linked to increased efficiency of the application, improved customer experience, or improved user journey to help improve sales.

- Incremental Channel Experience: Any improvements in channel experience or cross-channel experience, such as the introduction or improvement in mobile experience, web experience, or other channels.

- Customer Experience improvement: Clear metrics such as CSAT, NPS, and user journey durations to reach a call to action could be potential ways of measuring customer experience. Improvement in customer experience must also be linked to an increase in sales and brand reputation. Reducing customer churn could also be another significant metric, as retaining existing customers is often considered more profitable than acquiring new customers.

## Cost Levers:

While increasing revenue is one way, reducing costs also brings significant value to improving the bottom lines of large organizations.

Cost metrics that you could consider linking with your low-code/Citizen Development projects are as follows:

Productivity: This could be both time savings for employees or time saved on completing processes in the organization. Automation that reduces manual work, repetitive tasks, data entry tasks, removes process bottlenecks, increases self-service, and reduces manual intervention may all be common objectives of low code or Citizen Development projects and can be easily measured to show value and attributed to cost savings.

Technology Costs: Low-code projects are expected to reduce complexity, increase reusability, reduce training time, and also reduce time to launch. All of these should bring cost savings to the organization.

## Employee Experience:

While often organizations focus on customer experience, and that should certainly be a key focus area for any business, employees and their experiences across processes are equally critical.

Traditionally, enterprise applications have been lacking in providing end-user experience and ease of use, and this often adversely impacts the usage and adoption of systems in place. When employees do not make efficient use of the systems in place, it promotes offline record-keeping, loss of data, increases security risks, and reduces productivity.

Improving employee experience is, therefore, a key objective, and low-code and citizen development platforms can provide immense help with such use cases.

Key value metrics one can look at from an employee experience perspective are as follows:

- Employee Retention: An increase in employee retention is a great metric, but attribution to process and systems is an uphill task. Unless you have criteria that can be directly substantiated through employee surveys that vouch for retention rates, it would be advisable to avoid this metric.

- Employee experience: Measured in a similar fashion, same as customer experience through surveys and carefully crafted questions that they can answer anonymously without any fear.

# Chapter 10

# Operating Model

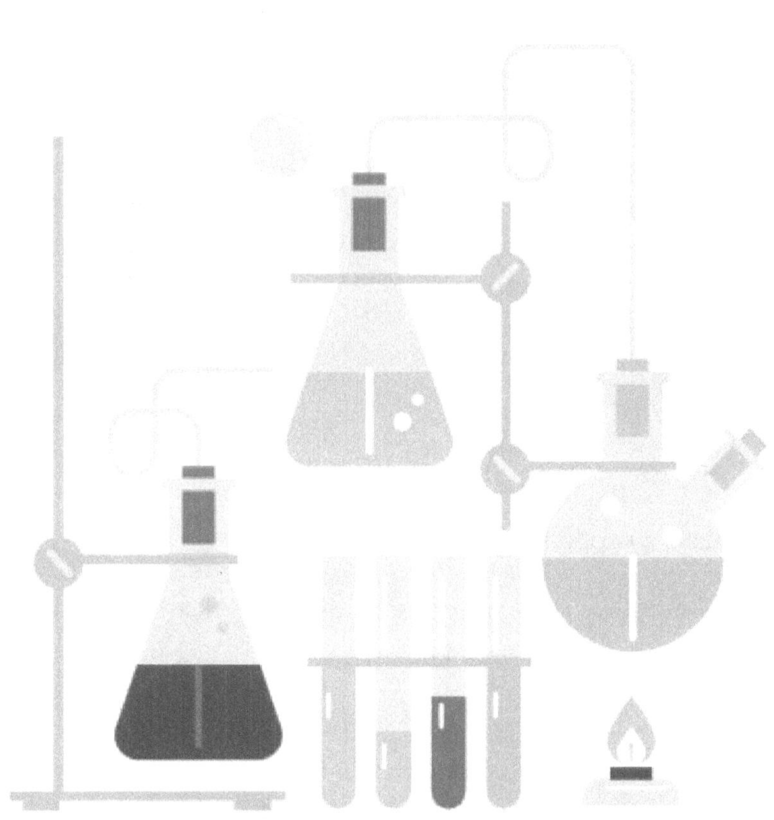

*The Strength of an Operating Model lies in
its ability to balance discipline and flexibility.*

There are three types of operating models that one could choose from. The choice of the model would depend on the structure of your organization.

## Centre of Excellence:

This model is usually chosen by hierarchical organizations. Such centers can either report into IT or be structured to report into a Common/Shared Business Operations unit.

Below are some of the salient features of this model:

- The structure would be more formal.

- Decisions would be on a top-down basis.

- Governance is more stringent with processes clearly laid down, documented, and approved.

- Any change to processes would be controlled and would need to be approved.

- Formal role descriptions are defined for all roles on the project.

- IT plays a supervisory role..

- Accountability and responsibilities are clearly documented, through a formal document such as the RACI matrix.

- Risks and Issues are clearly tracked and maintained using a formal document such as a RAID log.

- Performance measures and clearly documented and included as part of team objectives.

- Teams operating with this model are expected to have a good understanding of the processes, therefore training and knowledge transfer programs are in place for new joiners.

This model is well-suited for large organizations that already follow a very elaborate governance mechanism for their projects, the organization is more hierarchical and decisions flow from top to bottom.

Let's look at some pros and cons of this model:

| Pros | Cons |
| --- | --- |
| Well-suited to monitor compliance with policies and security | A high degree of control could stifle innovation and creativity. |
| Resources are allocated efficiently, and tracking usage is easier. | Higher risk of processes becoming bottlenecks. |
| Easier control and monitoring of activity. | Difficult for teams to adapt to changes. |
| Organized onboarding and offboarding of resources | Adapting agile approaches during execution is harder with deeper processes and formal role definitions. |
| Easier to establish centralized reusables, knowledge, and lessons learned. | |

# Community of Practice Model:

This model is generally adopted by organizations with a flat structure and that operate in a more nimble or agile fashion.

Below are some of the salient features of the Community of Practice model:

- The model is built to allow more freedom for teams that can independently perform units of work without much dependence on the larger organization or deep governance layers.

- Teams are given necessary resources such as time, budget, and scope boundaries to operate without much interference.

- Project methods are typically agile-driven.

- Management operates in a servant leadership fashion to enable rather than to control.

- Collaboration is a key aspect since it forms the bedrock of how teams operate, and if you are to follow this model, then investing in good collaboration tools would be a wise choice.

- Process and documentation requirements are at a bare minimum and evolve and need to have a basis within smaller functions or units rather than having to follow a formalised approach that is top-down driven.

- Objectives are iterative and evolving.

- Performance measures are outcome-based and broader.

Let's look at some pros and cons of this model:

| Pros | Cons |
|---|---|
| Model is less control-driven, hence promoting innovation. | Higher risk of losing control over compliance. |
| Easier for teams to operate and adapt to changes. | Unchecked growth on the platform may need frequent audits and cleansing to maintain quality. |
| Easier adoption of agile principles and approaches while executing projects. | Harder to impose direction on the whole organization when needed, as teams are operating in a more siloed fashion. |
| | Reusables are harder to generate as applications may not adhere to a common set of principles. |

## Hybrid Model:

The third model is the hybrid model that allows you to pick qualities from both models and use them as a new operating model that fits your organization and aligns with your priorities.

In this model, you would have both a Centre of Excellence as well as a community.

Therefore, it would be key to understand and clearly identify the responsibilities of the COE vs. the scope and boundaries of the communities.

The usual approach is to have a Centre of Excellence with a core set of employees who have a good understanding of the processes as well as are trained and experienced in the execution tools.

Along with these, the business teams loan resources as and when projects are commissioned in their respective departments or based on other conditions such as availability, skills, etc.

The loaned resources form part of a community that works on specific projects with a scope and budget and have control within the scope of that project. The COE also contributes one or more developers to the team, who not only contribute to the project but also ensure process adherence and compliance with policies.

Let's look at some pros and cons of this model:

| Pros | Cons |
| --- | --- |
| Provides a balance between control and innovation. | If the scope boundaries of COE and Community are not well-defined, it could lead to chaos. |
| Allows flexibility in operation and recalibration based on feedback. | |
| | |

# Chapter 11

# Case Study

*"Fairy tales are more than true – not because they tell us dragons exist, but because they tell us dragons can be beaten."*
G.K. Chesterton

Developing a Citizen Development practice is no dragon, and yet it is an uphill task and needs consistent efforts to be successful.

In this chapter, we will explore one such case where I had the opportunity to oversee the implementation of a Citizen Development practice personally. While I would not be able to reveal the organization's name or the people, I am sharing the learnings here from the practical application of what we have read so far.

The routine of selecting a platform and getting to the first project and having that completed is not a challenge for most organizations. We do that day in and day out with other kinds of software and systems. We only need to keep in mind the factors mentioned in the book while we go through that exercise.

Establishing governance for citizen development in a large organization, on the other hand, is not common. Very few organizations have attempted it, and fewer have been successful to my knowledge.

We will look at a customer who is currently on that path, and we will specifically look at what they did to establish the operating model.

For the sake of convenience, we name the organization ABC Corp.

ABC Corp is a large enterprise with operations in over 14 countries, spanning three continents. It has two main operations – a medical equipment dealership and a service business - to serve customers for the equipment or parts sold.

ABC Corp already had a citizen development platform under its portfolio of applications. It was procured a few years back to manage the procurement processes of one of the business units.

The procurement team, while onboarding the platform, did not explore the no code or citizen development capabilities. Rather, they only chose the platform for its procurement application that seemed to have prebuilt processes that were easily customizable to the specific needs of the organization, had a user-friendly UI, and was able to integrate efficiently with the ERP for invoice processing and other functions.

Having used the platform for procurement at one BU, the simplicity of the application helped it expand into other BUs in the organization.

The IT team, however, was aware of its capabilities and wanted to expand the use cases on the platform beyond procurement.

This is where they needed help:

- How to approach the business teams?

- What use cases to begin with, as here they would have to propose use cases?

- How to convince the top management to allow business teams and users from different departments to build processes for the identified use cases?

- How to measure the success of the applications built?

- How to train more users after the first set of processes is built?

- How to ensure data security and other compliance requirements are not violated?

And finally, how to set up a model to ensure the growth of platform usage and the number of citizen developers increases gradually across business units and countries in a self-sustaining fashion.

While it was an uphill task, the IT team had one advantage. No one had asked them to set this up, and the platform costs were already justified by the procurement processes.

The IT team began with finance, as the CIO had a good rapport with the CFO, and the CFO saw value in the platform, if not for the larger organization, then for his own team.

The finance team was running several processes outside the system, manually using Excel sheets, and running approvals through emails. It was getting difficult to track many of these transactions without their history, and having to search through emails every time was painful.

Also, during audits, both internal and external, such ad hoc, out-of-the-system processes could be considered a risk.

The finance team identified a set of ten processes to start with, including compliance, risk, invoice approval, supplier onboarding, and proforma invoice review processes.

The IT team ensured that some of the processes included have a larger end-user base to ensure that the platform gets used by more users, hence enabling word of mouth and first-hand experience of the platform's ease of use and ease of build.

ABC Corp's Project Management Office had primarily operated on a conventional SDLC/waterfall-based approach to run projects. However, on this initiative, the CIO obtained buy-in from the top management and the PMO to use Scrum.

All the requirements were charted into a product backlog, and the citizen developers identified, along with the Scrum Master and Product Owner (both from the IT organization), decided on the scope of the first sprint and started work.

After initial hiccups around access, collaboration issues, and confusion on who should do what, the team settled down within a week, and the first sprint was completed in 2 weeks' time, with a positive "Done" list that was more than the initial requirements on the sprint backlog.

The team was underconfident and hesitant, hence they had estimated the requirements for Sprint one in a conservative fashion.

After the first sprint, the team felt more confident and was ready to take on more work as part of Sprint 2.

After four sprints, all the processes identified were delivered and also launched incrementally for end-user consumption.

Although the team realized some gaps in the process design post-launch that were rectified swiftly, the overall impact of the project was significant.

The whole management, PMO, and all stakeholders involved appreciated the quick yet high-quality delivery of the applications and processes.

The team was highly motivated and ready to take on more work as citizen developers.

Word of mouth spread of the success of the project, the swift automation, and most importantly that business teams had themselves solved problems that had been pending for many years, with little help from the IT organization.

The CEO nudged other directors and VPs under him to also actively encourage their teams to try this new, simple yet efficient platform to solve their issues.

The IT team was jubilant, but they were still the gatekeepers of this initiative, and the next challenge was about to hit them.

The IT team started receiving a lot of queries from various departments across countries to use the platform for some of their requirements. Some of these departments also demanded that their teams be quickly trained on the platform so they can build their own processes.

The Procurement team, which was the owner of the platform until now as the core procurement processes ran on the same platform, was concerned about the onslaught of activity on the platform and whether their processes would be impacted by changes or new processes being introduced and the possibility of performance impacts.

The IT team was overwhelmed. There was org-wide visibility, and the top management was supportive of the initiative. It was the perfect time to move forward. But they hadn't thought things would turn around so fast. They wanted to see through the successful implementation of the pilot and use that to learn and improve the process for the next project. They had to consider all the factors before them and decide on the future course of action.

- What do we do with the piling requests for inclusions in the next project?

- How do we evaluate if the requirements fit the capability of the platform?

- How do we train so many new users from each of the departments?

- How do we give them access in a way that data security across other processes, either live or in build, is not impacted?

- How do we run so many different projects at the same time?

- How do we ensure there are no performance issues?

- How do we plan for release management?

- How would testing of all these new processes be carried out?

- With all these open questions, it was certain that they could not open up the floodgates now to all queries, as that would do more harm than good. But they needed to inform the teams in such a way that they were not discouraged.

- This brings them to the last How-to – How do we communicate?

Let's look at how we tackled these questions:

We took the suitability assessment templates from PMI and modified them to include specific compliance and NFR requirements of ABC Corp. We created a quick form on the citizen development platform to submit requests by answering questions on an assessment.

The assessment was built in with questions, answers, and weights assigned to each question and answer choices.

Based on the online submissions, the requests that scored high on the criteria for Citizen Development were then sent for a second-level committee review that would then revalidate the requirements and sort them on a priority list.

This priority list was then sorted into different buckets. Each bucket of requests would be handed over to one community of citizen developers that was closer to that bucket in terms of business process familiarity, location, and skills.

Five different such communities were established to start with, which would pick up 50 processes over the next two months for delivery in an agile fashion.

The committee approving requests sat within a Shared COE, which also trained and allocated product owners and Scrum Masters for each of the communities.

All citizen developers received platform training and Scrum training before beginning work within their respective communities.

Each of the communities had its independence in terms of scope and running the Sprint planning, sprint backlogs, and retrospectives. The communities also managed their own definition of done; however, the NFRs were provided by the COE.

Post the Sprint reviews, the accepted "Done" items of the backlog were moved to a common Release Backlog that was shared between all the communities.

The release backlog was managed by the COE to ensure releases were planned without impacting currently active applications and without downtime impact on current processes and users.

The release backlog process was a cautious step that was put in place to cover any risks, but depending on how your platform structures releases and rollbacks, you may or may not need this step.

Each of the communities had its own development space that was segregated within the instance, and access could be segregated based on this space. The platform also allowed the promotion of changes from the development space on one environment to the next, so there was automated promotion of code from the development instance to the test instance to the production instance without manual interference.

Regression test scripts were put in place to test any impact on existing artifacts every time there was a new release, which meant that any impact due to the incremental changes was captured and addressed immediately post go-lives.

ABC Corp used a collaboration tool that allowed one-on-one chat, group chat, and also allowed people to share ideas and content with a larger audience to collaborate and communicate. This helped in collaborating within communities, between communities, and also between communities and the COE. It also helped communicate and appreciate success across the organization since all of ABC Corp used the same collaboration platform.

You will notice that we set up a hybrid model here with the COE and the communities.

Most often in practical situations, it would seem as if hybrid is the only choice, but you may decide to structure it differently.

My personal sense was that ABC Corp had functioned with traditional delivery models for a long time, and for them to suddenly change to a hybrid model that is very open would be difficult.

Although we ended up with a strong COE, considering the nature of ABC Corp, the structure we put in place was very forward-looking.

With time, as the platform grows, the COE probably will release more control to the communities on how work is chosen, delivered, and released. For now, it is a model that works and allows for growth without chaos.

You would also notice that with this operating model, we answered all of the questions that challenged us at the beginning of this exercise.

# Chapter 12

# Industry Use cases

*Birds of a feather flock together.*

We often like to see references from our own industry/domain. Competitors trying to replicate successful business strategies is not new.

We are without a doubt already in the early majority stage with respect to adoption of low-code, no code, and citizen development platforms.

Early adopters have already shown the way on possible use cases in different industries and domains. There are also plenty of case studies highlighting challenges faced, ROI, and methodology used.

Moreover, there are now many vendors in the market who have successfully delivered enterprise-grade solutions using low code, no code to solve various problems and have the experience to replicate the success.

Let's explore a few use cases based on industry types and domains:

## BFSI:

1. **Customer Onboarding & KYC**: Customer onboarding and KYC processes often become cumbersome for banks and other financial services and insurance companies. Different projects may have different onboarding process flows, data requirements, and KYC. This information also changes frequently.

   As such, having rigid, unresponsive systems is not effective. Low-code apps could solve this challenge by enabling business teams to manage processes and experience per product/region. The front end in this case would be managed outside of this setup and integrate with the app driving processes, rules.

This headless approach of separating UI and underlying processes ensures flexibility and scalability without impacting the end-user experience.

2.  **Loan Origination Process:** Loan management itself has several facets. Loan origination is one of the first. Loan origination includes several steps starting from data collection through different channels, to underwriting, to approvals, to review, and then the final award of the loan products to the customers.

    This process again becomes complicated and difficult to change with traditional approaches.

    New policies, rules, and checks are placed incrementally based on environmental factors, and this needs to be updated into the rule engines quickly.

    Since organizations are not nimble enough in the ability to update what they have created, many of the processes in the loan origination stage become manual.

    Low Code/No Code can effectively give the power of automation back to the business teams for them to quickly organize and automate processes, change based on regulations and policy, update rules for approvals, etc.

3.  **Risk and Compliance:** Risk and compliance related processes are often not supported by out-of-the-box enterprise applications for BFSI. Often, risk and compliance officers struggle to manage their inspection and compliance routines in organizations.

    With low code, such processes can be automated based on the needs of your own organization.

# Manufacturing:

1.  **Quality Management**: Quality-related processes on traditional ERP software tend to be simplified and often do not cater to the variations and complexity that prevail when managing quality within manufacturing organizations.

    With Low code, you can not only tailor the processes that you need in your organization to ensure quality standards are met, but you can also easily use a headless framework to enable the processes into a front end, such as a mobile app, for easy handling on the floor.

2.  **Maintenance Management:** While maintenance processes are available on most traditional ERP solutions, they miss key components relating to execution. They often tend to be rigid and less end-user friendly for a field/floor scenario, which needs a more modern, sleek, and easy UI to allow for quick allocation, dynamic decision making, recording of readings, and subsequent process triggers based on the readings.

    Use the low-code apps on top of your ERP to achieve a more comprehensive automation of your maintenance processes and handovers between processes, such as preventive maintenance checks, inspections, work orders, and root cause analysis reporting.

3.  **Shop floor Management:** Traditional ERPs are transactional systems that do very well when you want to capture what happened.

    Automation is all about having a system that enables the "how." Shop Floor, again, is not a setup where one can use laptops or desktops to enter transactional data.

Mobile-based process enablement to manage different processes with end-user experience in mind is key. Be it managing inspection checklists,

Completing protocols for initiation and release, handing over from one process to another. All these could be automated with low code in an efficient manner. IoT and integration could be enabled to reduce manual intervention and increase more tightly coupled handovers.

## Retail & Hospitality:

1.  **Category Management**: Category Management for large retail or distributor organisations is one of those processes that is both unique to each organisation and industry. It is important to understand the processes carefully and build something that is both scalable and flexible. Low code is best suited for such applications.

    Added advantage here is the ability of such platforms to quickly enable processes for different user groups. Ranging from category managers to procurement teams, finance teams, and vendors.

    Each of the groups is shown and given access to only the sections they need access to.

2.  Hotels can use low-code platforms to manage key processes such as managing service and maintenance requests, hotel reservations, and simple, easy-to-use guest self-service and experience processes that ease the load and help organise the work.

The ease of use of the self-service-driven processes helps immensely as the end users are a floating group that cannot be trained to use new apps and hence the experience needs to be extremely easy.

3.  Loyalty Management is another key use case that needs careful design based on several inputs, points calculations, process flows to manage campaigns, approvals, and a headless application that can easily interact with several front-end channels and back-end sources to collect and serve data.

## Real Estate:

1.  **Construction Project Management:** Real Estate Companies often have elaborate project management needs, but most project management applications available are tailored towards software project management and cannot easily adhere to construction use cases.

    Material Management, Tasks, and Quality Management are key sections, but many times there might be process and approval cycles within tasks. When there are different lifecycles for tasks based on task types or other such constraints, existing systems struggle to support it, and such tasks are often tracked and completed outside the system, and only final transaction entries go into the system.

    We need systems that can help in actual execution and that are also available for use in the field.

    As such, low code platforms are best suited to address this need.

2. **Quality Management**: Construction quality management processes, like those we saw earlier in the case of manufacturing, are unique to the industry, region, and the company.

   Ensuring adherence to policy and quality standards, inspection mechanisms, schedules, action plans based on inspections and check results, tracking risks and mitigation plans are all important and critical processes that often run outside the system.

3. **Maintenance Management**: Real estate organisations often struggle with property maintenance solutions post-delivery. Like manufacturing more than the transactions, enabling the organization to run with an ease to use, integrated, mobile-friendly, and flexible application is key.

   Low-code applications are very well poised to handle this use case.

## Automotive Dealers:

1. **Equipment Service & Maintenance:** This is another area where the service processes are dependent on the structure and processes provided by OEMs.

   While the OEMs provide guidelines on the operating model, day-to-day execution is left to the dealer.

   The result is a heavily customized solution with tight integrations, or a process that runs manually to a large extent.

   Low-Code apps would provide the necessary flexibility here to quickly build flexible and scalable processes that can also align with OEM models and operating procedures and integrate with them.

A lot of the other processes we have mentioned for previous domains, such as quality management and project management, also apply here.

Of course, with the industry flavors differing from one domain to the other, the essence remains the same.

## Healthcare & Pharma:

1. **Patient Journey/Experience:** Patient Experience has many facets. The types of requests could be both emergency and non-emergency. Requests could be coming in from various channels.

   Triaging incoming requests, appointment scheduling based on doctor availability, or taking the patients or guests through a journey in the clinic or hospital is a process that needs to be crafted meticulously.

   The process may include various steps that traverse through different departments – from registration, collecting basic information such as height, weight, vital checks, routing to available physicians, recording diagnosis, prescription printing, handing over to insurance provider APIs for eligibility checks, and then finally offboarding.

   Most enterprise applications for hospitals are good record-keeping systems or transaction systems. Use a low-code app that can sit on top of the EMR systems and fetch necessary information to facilitate an easy and fast patient onboarding experience.

2.  **Pharma QMS:** The Pharma Industry has a very elaborate and specific Quality Management Processes, and the QMS systems must adhere to strict regulations.

    Such systems are usually custom-built by organizations. Low code would be an excellent fit to explore. It can help create flexible systems that adhere to regulations, incorporate specific processes for quality checks, audits, test procedures, non-conformance action plans and processes, change control, deviation control among others.

## Oil & Gas:

Many of the use cases we have seen already, such as quality management, maintenance, and project management, could be very good fits for the oil and gas industry as well.

In addition to this, following are some more use cases to consider:

1.  **HSE: Health, Safety, and Environment;** While this is a key process or function for oil and gas companies, it may be applicable to other organisations involved in manufacturing also.

    Health and Safety procedures need to be followed carefully across the org, both during business as Usual and during emergency situations.

    Regular inspections, action plans based on inspection trigger points, quality checks of HSE equipment, and training-related processes are some examples of processes that could be automated as part of the application.

2.  **ESG**: Environment-related processes such as ESG reporting, data collection, processes to perform material assessment, goal setting, tracking, task tracking and completion, reporting, and analytics are picking up rapidly.

    Scope 1, 2, 3 calculations based on various data points, GHG emissions, and carbon footprint data collection, consolidation, and reporting are rapidly becoming talking points across boardrooms.

These are, again, industry-, region-, and company-driven processes and metrics, and one-size-fits-all applications cannot help.

Low code can do wonders for automation in this space that is growing rapidly.

## Government & Citizen Services:

Governments and public sector companies are exploring low code in a big way.

A lot of the government organizations have not been able to fully capitalize on the cloud journey due to regulatory constraints and have a legacy systems problem that they would like to solve, but have been waiting for options to open up.

With low-code frameworks being available both on public cloud, private cloud, and on-premise models, public sector companies now see an opportunity to move their legacy applications and modernize them to a more flexible, scalable, user-friendly UI-based solutions.

Some key use cases to start with:

1. **Citizen Services:** Online applications or forms with massive volumes that need filtration, case management based on criteria, routing, and resolution are excellent use cases to start with.

   This could be any kind of service ranging from visas or license provisioning to citizen grievance redressal systems.

   The core advantage lies in the fact that all these processes are prone to policy changes, and those changes must be reflected in the applications quickly to ensure faster enforcement of changes according to the latest laws of the land.

   This could be automated with low code, helping agencies to manage the changes easily and effectively.

2. **Risk and Compliance:** Automation of risk and compliance processes within public sector organisations is very specific and may be confidential in many ways.

   Automation of these processes is key to ensuring transparency and consistency in policy communication, application, and measuring adherence.

   This may also include processes where employees can quickly request or check their actions or future actions for policy compliance, initiate approvals, or manage compliance checklists.

While these are just a couple of examples, legacy modernization with public sector organizations using low code could find many use cases, since off-the-shelf applications rarely fit in with the specific processes in place.

# Chapter 13

## Conclusion

*The end that is the beginning.*

In the chapters above, we have seen a case study applying citizen development and other set of use cases with different industries.

One must not look at the power of low code only from the prism of the use cases mentioned in the previous chapter.

The opportunities with low code in your company or industry are many. You must follow the methods prescribed in the book to evaluate possible use cases; only that will help you identify the right use cases for your company.

With ABC Corp, we had the advantage of the platform already being in use, easy access, and buy-in from the top management. However, the larger business teams needed guidance and direction. Hence, a COE model was essential to provide that guidance and pillar of support.

In several other organizations, I see that the business is active not only in running their own initiatives but also deploying their own systems, leading to a severe shadow IT problem.

In such organizations, you would do well to set up a model where the business teams have more power and IT oversees more of the compliance, security, and governance aspects only, but does not control or dictate what is to be done.

While we explored citizen development, low code-driven practices may need a different approach where IT still plays a larger role in actual contribution to development.

Every organization's journey would be different; you might face different challenges. But as long as you stick to the basic principles and then build on them based on your needs, you will be able to make progress.

Digitization and process automation are fast-changing the world. It is imperative that we equip ourselves with all the necessary tools to allow faster growth and increase productivity and efficiency.

Citizen Development and low-code platforms provide the much-needed breathing space for large enterprises to transform and find value faster.

With this, we come to the end of the book. Hopefully, this is also where your organization's Low Code No Code journey begins.

**The End**